Mark D C McKinnon   Almudena Sáiz García

Mark D C McKinnon

Profesor de inglés en la Escuela de Idiomas Modernos de la Universitat Autónoma de Barcelona, formador de profesores en Oxford TEFL

Almudena Sáiz García

Licenciada en filología inglesa por la Universidad de Salamanca, y actual profesora de español como lengua extranjera en Olé Languages

director de la colección: **Eduard Sancho**
autores: **Mark D C McKinnon, Almudena Sáiz García**
diseño de la cubierta: **La japonesa**
diseño del interior: **La japonesa**
ilustraciones: **Sergi Padró**
agradecimientos: **Victoria Aragonés, Stuart Lewis, Kyle Mawer, Graham Stanley, Blanca Moreno y nuestras familias y amigos.**

© Difusión, Centro de Investigación y Publicaciones de Idiomas, S.L.,
Barcelona, 2009
Reimpresión: marzo 2010
ISBN: 978-84-8443-577-8
depósito legal: B-14.112-2010
impreso en España por Novoprint

C/ Trafalgar, 10, entlo. 1ª
08010 Barcelona
Tel. (+34) 93 268 03 00
Fax (+34) 93 310 33 40
editorial@difusion.com

www.difusion.com

Hoy en día resultaría casi un disparate no aprender inglés. Lengua global de comunicación de nuestros días, el inglés es también el idioma de las nuevas tecnologías y de los soportes multimedia como internet, los móviles o los juegos de ordenador. Vivimos en un mundo en constante evolución, por lo que es de vital importancia estar al día, reciclarse, conocer las nuevas tendencias y saber usar los términos que las identifican. En definitiva, aprender a entender este mundo moderno y cambiante en el que vivimos.

De este convencimiento surge la necesidad de crear una guía práctica, de consulta fácil, para ayudar a entender las palabras y expresiones más útiles, habituales y curiosas de la lengua popular, tanto del inglés británico como del americano. **Word up!** recoge términos que en general no aparecen ni en los diccionarios convencionales ni en los libros de texto, bien porque son tabú, políticamente incorrectos o simplemente porque son de reciente creación. Esta obra pretende divertir e interesar al lector con temas y términos actuales y prácticos (argot, neologismos, acrónimos, coloquialismos, etc.) extraídos de fuentes reales: series de TV, chats, películas y, sobre todo, de la calle.

Word up! es, en definitiva, un pequeño diccionario dirigido a todos aquellos hispanohablantes que sientan necesidad o curiosidad por este tipo de lenguaje. Por su estructura bidireccional, es ideal también para todos los hablantes de inglés que quieran acercarse al español auténtico que se utiliza hoy en día.

Los autores

Abreviaturas utilizadas en

abrev.	abreviatura
acron.	acrónimo
adj.	adjetivo
adv.	adverbio
expr.	expresión
interj.	interjección
loc.	locución (nominal o verbal)
loc. adv.	locución adverbial
n.	nombre
pl.	plural
UK	propio del Reino Unido
USA	propio de los Estados Unidos
v.	verbo
v. prnl.	verbo pronominal
vul.	vulgar

ENGLISH-ESPAÑOL

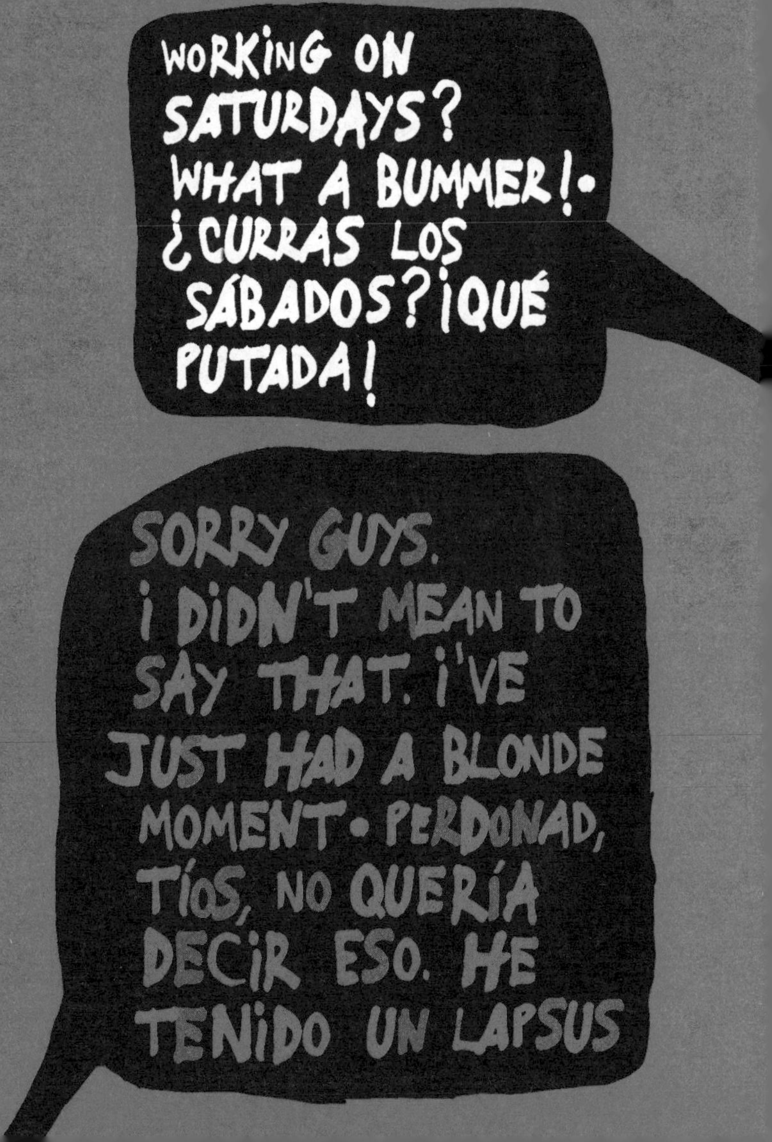
WORKING ON SATURDAYS? WHAT A BUMMER!. ¿CURRAS LOS SÁBADOS? ¡QUÉ PUTADA!
SORRY GUYS. I DIDN'T MEAN TO SAY THAT. I'VE JUST HAD A BLONDE MOMENT. PERDONAD, TÍOS, NO QUERÍA DECIR ESO. HE TENIDO UN LAPSUS

10 minutes ago
PASADO (DE MODA), DEL AÑO DE LA PERA

—*That is so 10 minutes ago!* • *¡Eso está tan pasado!*

10-4
MENSAJE RECIBIDO
Pertenece a la jerga policial, pero es de uso muy común.

—*Office: Any taxi for Main Street? It's urgent.// Taxi driver: 10-4. I'm on my way.* • *Central: ¿Hay algún taxi para Main Street? Es urgente.// Taxista: Mensaje recibido. Estoy en camino.*

187
ASESINATO
Expresión que proviene de la jerga policial.

—*I need back-up. We got a 187 here.* • *Necesito refuerzos. Ha habido un asesinato.*

2 cents [USA]
OPINIÓN, GRANITO DE ARENA

—*Let me get my 2 cents in here!* • *¡Déjame que diga algo sobre eso!*

24/7
LAS 24 HORAS DEL DÍA (24 HORAS AL DÍA, 7 DÍAS A LA SEMANA)

—*We're watching the suspect 24/7.* • *Estamos vigilando al sospechoso las 24 horas del día.*

4U *acron.*
(for you)
PARA TI
4 es la abreviación de **for** y **u**, de **you**. Estas abreviaciones se usan mucho en SMS, en chats y en canciones pop.

—*Kisses 4u.* • *Besos para ti.*

411 [USA]
INFORMACIÓN, NOTICIAS, DATOS
La expresión viene del número de teléfono de información.

—*Look at that chick! I need the 411 on her.* • *¡Mira a esa tía! Necesito información sobre ella.*

6s and 7s (to be at)
ESTAR BLOQUEADO/A, NO DAR PIE CON BOLA

—*The defence was at 6s and 7s. We lost 6-0.* • *La defensa no dio pie con bola. Perdimos 6 a 0.*

9 to 5
CURRO

—*I have a new 9 to 5 at the local supermarket. I'm so happy.* • *Tengo un nuevo curro en el supermercado del barrio. Estoy muy contento.*

ace *adj., expr.*

1 LO MÁS, DE PUTA MADRE

—*That movie is **ace**.* • *Esa peli es lo más.*

2 ¡DE PUTA MADRE!

—*Julian: I got tickets for the gig,* // *Graham: **Ace**, man!* • *Julian: Tengo entradas para el concierto.* // *Graham: ¡De puta madre, tío!*

act up *v.*

1 ARMARLA, PORTARSE MAL (ESPECIALMENTE LOS NIÑOS)

—*Mum: Kids, stop **acting up**, or you'll be going to bed.* • *Mamá: Niños, como no dejéis de armarla, os vais a la cama.*

2 ESCACHARRARSE

—*This rust bucket is **acting up** again.* • *Esta tartana se está escacharrando otra vez.*

action (get) *loc.*

MOJAR, PILLAR CACHO

—*Duncan: Did you **get** any **action** at the weekend?* // *Pete: No, the disco was full of mingers.* • *Duncan: ¿Mojaste este finde?* // *Pete: No, la disco estaba llena de cardos.*

afaik *acron.*

(as far as I know)

QUE YO SEPA

—*Does she have msn?* // ***afaik**, no* • *¿Tiene messenger?* // *Que yo sepa, no.*

ain't *v.*

Contracción negativa del verbo **be** en presente. Por ejemplo: **I am not** = **I ain't**, **You are not** = **You ain't**, etc.

air biscuit *n.*

PEDO

—*I smell an **air biscuit**!* • *¡Aquí huele a pedo!*

aka *acron.*

(also known as)

TAMBIÉN CONOCIDO COMO
Usado para indicar los apodos o sobrenombres por los que se conoce a una persona o algo en general.

—*Bruce Springsteen **aka** "The Boss".* • *Bruce Springsteen también conocido como "El Boss".*

alcopops *n.*
Especie de cubata embotellado. Normalmente lo toman las chicas. No aptos para **real men**.

all right (a bit of) *expr.*
COMO UN TREN, MUY BUENO/A
—Daniel's *a bit of all right*. • Daniel está como un tren.

and stuff *expr.*
Y TAL, Y ESO
Se usa para añadir un término poco preciso, pero semejante a lo ya dicho. Característico de personas que no tienen mucho don de palabra y no saben cómo terminar las frases.
—I like bikes, cars *and stuff*. • Me gustan las motos, los coches y tal.

anorak [UK] *n.*
FRIQUI
—Eddie's working on his stamp collection. He's a complete *anorak*. • Eddie está trabajando en su colección de sellos. Es un friqui total.

argy bargy *n.*
JALEO, BRONCA, FOLLÓN
—There was a bit of *argy bargy* in the pub last night. • Hubo un poco de jaleo en el pub ayer.

arse licker *n.*
LAMECULOS, PELOTA
—He only got the promotion because he was an *arselicker*. • Le ascendieron porque es un lameculos.

asap *acron.*
(as soon as possible)
CUANTO ANTES
—Answer me *asap*. • Contéstame cuanto antes.

at the minute *loc. adv.*
AHORA MISMO
—I can't talk to you *at the minute*. • No puedo hablar contigo ahora mismo.

awol *acron.*
(absent without leave)
DESAPARECIDO/A EN COMBATE, MISSING
—Michael's gone *awol* again. • Michael está missing otra vez.

OTRA EXPRESIÓN QUE SIGNIFICA LO MISMO Y QUE TAMBIÉN PROVIENE DE LA JERGA MILITAR ES MIA (MISSING IN ACTION)

b4 *acron.*
(before)
ANTES

—*Seen U **B4**.* • *Te he visto antes.*

En inglés escrito, en un registro informal como en los sms o en los chats, se usan muchas expresiones formadas por letras y números que fonéticamente suenan igual que las palabras referidas. Por ejemplo, **b** (**be**) **4** (**four**) = **before** y **U** = **you**.

baconify *v.*
PONER BACON

—*Can you **baconify** my burger, please?* • *¿Me pones bacon en la hamburguesa, por favor?*

bad business *n.*
1 ASUNTO CHUNGO

—*He's just got into some **bad business**.* • *Se acaba de meter en algún asunto chungo.*

2 PERSONA CHUNGA

—*That guy is **bad business**.* • *Ese tío es un chungo.*

bad hair day *n.*
UN DÍA EN EL QUE SALE TODO MAL, UN MAL DÍA

—*What's wrong with her? // She's having a **bad hair day**.* • *¿Qué le pasa? // Tiene un mal día.*

badass [USA] *adj.*
Badass puede referirse tanto a algo "muy bueno" como "muy malo", dependiendo del contexto y de la intención.

—*He's a **badass** mofo.* • *Es un hijo de puta de mucho cuidado.*

—*Jimmy has this **badass** moustache.* • *Jimmy tiene un pedazo de bigote.*

bail out *v.*
PAGAR LA DEUDA DE ALGUIEN, LIBERAR A ALGUIEN BAJO FIANZA

—*The government is **bailing out** the banks.* • *El gobierno está pagando las deudas de los bancos.*

bait *n.*

1 TÍA BUENA, PIBÓN

—*Let's go out and get some **bait**.* •
Salgamos a por pibones.

2 jail bait *n.*

LOLITA, MENOR DE EDAD

—*Careful, man! She's **jail bait**!*
• *¡Cuidado, tío! ¡Es menor de edad!*

baller [USA] *n.*

1 BUEN JUGADOR DE BASKET

—*That boy's a **baller**.* • *Ese chaval
es un crack del basket.*

2 TRIUNFADOR/A

—*That ghetto boy's a **baller** now.
He's made it big time.* • *Ese chaval
de barrio ha triunfado a saco.*

ballin' *adj.*

FORRADO/A, MONTADO/A
EN EL DÓLAR, QUE LO TIRA

—*Bill Gates is **ballin'**.* • *Bill Gates
está forrao.*

balls *n. pl., expr.*

1 COJONES, HUEVOS

—*He didn't have the **balls** to do it.*
• *No tuvo cojones para hacerlo.*

2 ¡JODER!

—***Balls**! I've had enough!* • *¡Joder!
¡Estoy harto!*

balls up *v., n.*

1 CAGARLA, JODERLA

—*Shit! I've **ballsed** it **up** again!*
• *¡Mierda! ¡La he vuelto a cagar!*

2 CAGADA

—*What a **balls up**!* • *¡Qué cagada!*

ballistic (go) *loc.*

PILLAR UN BUEN CABREO

—*He **went ballistic** when we told
him.* • *Se pilló un buen cabreo cuando se lo dijimos.*

baltic *adj.*

UN FRÍO QUE PELA

—*Oh, man. It's **baltic** out there.* •
Joder, tío, fuera hace un frío que pela.

bamboozle *v.*

LIAR, TOMAR EL PELO, TIMAR

—*OK, you give me 10, I'll give you
2, then you give your 2 to her and
that's us quits. Got that? || Erm...
you're **bamboozling** me.* • *Vale,
dame 10, yo te doy 2, entonces tú le
das 2 a ella, y estamos en paz. ¿Vale?
|| Mmm... Me estás liando.*

bang *interj., v.*

1 ¡PUM! (ALGO QUE PASA DE
REPENTE)

—*And **bang**! He was gone!* •
Y ¡pum!, se fue.

2 TIRARSE A ALGUIEN *(vul.)*

—*Hey dude! Are you **banging** my sister?* • *Eh, tío, ¿te estás tirando a mi hermana?*

bangin' *adj.*

1 PARA PERSONAS: ESTAR BUENO/A

—*Look at that, man. She's **bangin'**!* • *Mira eso, tío. ¡Qué buena está!*

2 PARA COSAS: ALUCINANTE, DE PUTA MADRE

—*This party's **bangin'**!* • *¡Esta fiesta está de puta madre!*

bank on *v.*

CONTAR CON, CONFIAR EN

—*Mike: Will we finish by 8, Joe? // Joe: I'm **banking on** it.* • *Mike: ¿Habremos terminado a las 8, Joe? // Joe: En principio, sí.*

barf *v.*

POTAR

—*He's had too much to drink. He's just **barfed**.* • *Ha bebido demasiado. Acaba de potar.*

barfaroni *adj.*

¡QUÉ ASCO!

—*Oh, **barfaroni**! I can't believe you're eating that shit!* • *¡Qué asco! ¡Cómo te puedes comer eso!*

barking mad *adj.*

MUY PIRADO/A, COMO UNA CABRA, FATAL

—*Mad? He's **barking mad**, mate.* • *¿Pirado? Está como una cabra, tío.*

bb *acron.*
(baby)

CARIÑO

—*I love U, **bb**.* • *Te quiero, cariño.*

bbiab *acron.*
(be back in a bit)

VUELVO ENSEGUIDA

—*tel. **BBIAB**.* • *tlf. Vuelvo enseguida.*

bbl *acron.*
(be back later)

VUELVO MÁS TARDE

—*Studying. **BBL**.* • *Estoy estudiando. Vuelvo más tarde.*

b-boy *n.*

Término para referirse a una persona que se identifica con la cultura hip-hop. También existe **b-girl**.

bbw *acron.*
(big beautiful woman)

EUFEMISMO PARA DESIGNAR A MUJERES GORDITAS Y HERMOSAS

—*I love you baby, you're my **bbw**.* • *Te quiero cari, tú eres mi gordita.*

beat up v.
DAR UNA PALIZA, PARTIRLE
LA CARA A ALGUIEN

—*Shut up Michael or I'll* **beat** *you* **up!** • *¡Cállate Michael o te parto la cara!*

beats me interj.
NI IDEA, NI FLORES

—*Woman: What is that? // Man:* **Beats me!** • *Mujer: ¿Qué es eso? // Hombre: ¡Ni idea!*

beau n.
LIGUE, ROLLITO

—*In this photo here we can see Madonna and her new* **beau**. • *En esta foto de aquí se ve a Madonna con su nuevo ligue.*

bed v.
ACOSTARSE CON ALGUIEN

—*He says he* **bedded** *10 000 women before he finally settled down with Carla.* • *Dice que se acostó con 10 000 mujeres antes de sentar la cabeza con Carla.*

bee's knees n.
LA HOSTIA, LA LECHE, LO MÁS

—*Our kid thinks he's the* **bee's knees** *but he's a loser.* • *Mi hermano se cree que es la hostia pero es un pringao.*

beef up v.
INTENSIFICAR, REFORZAR

—*We need to* **beef up** *our campaign or we'll lose.* • *Tenemos que intensificar nuestra campaña o perderemos.*

beer goggles n.
Fenómeno "paranormal" producido bajo los efectos del alcohol por el cual uno pierde todo criterio a la hora de buscar o elegir pareja sexual. (**Goggles** son gafas.)

—*She looked much better last night when I had my* **beer goggles** *on.* • *Estaba más buena anoche cuando llevaba mis "beer goggles".*

beer scooter n.
Fenómeno "paranormal" producido bajo los mismos efectos que el anterior; esta vez consiste en despertarse después de una noche "dura" sin saber cómo has llegado a casa. (**Scooter** es moto.)

—*I can't remember a thing, I must've got home on my* **beer scooter**. • *No me acuerdo de nada, habré llegado a casa en mi "beer scooter".*

beer belly n.
BARRIGA CERVECERA

—*Is that a* **beer belly** *I see?* • *¿Veo una barriga cervecera?*

bender (to go on a) loc.
SALIR DE FIESTA LOCA

—*Pete: Where have you been? // Dan:*

Sorry, man. **I went on a bender.**
• *Pete: ¿Dónde has estado? //Dan: Lo siento, tío. Me fui de fiesta y se lió bastante.*

bent *adj.*

1 CORRUPTO/A

—*He's a* **bent** *copper.* • *Es un poli corrupto.*

2 MARICA *(vul.)*

—*Sam's* **bent**. • *Sam es marica.*

bevvy *n.*

COPA, BEBIDA

—*We're going for a* **bevvy**. *Coming?* • *Nos vamos a tomar una copa. ¿Te vienes?*

bible thumper *n.*

CRISTIANO/A RADICAL, PREDICADOR/A PUERTA A PUERTA

—*Don't open the door! It's the* **bible thumpers!** • *¡No abras la puerta, que son los predicadores!*

bimbo *n.*

BARBIE

—*Samantha's such a* **bimbo**! • *¡Samantha es una barbie!*

bird [UK] *n.*

PIBA, CHURRI, CHAVALA

—*Hey Leonard, have you seen that new* **bird** *in accounts?* • *Leonard,*

¿has visto a la nueva churri de contabilidad?

black out *v.*

PERDER EL CONOCIMIENTO, DESMAYARSE

—*I can't remember a thing. I must've* **blacked out**. • *No recuerdo nada. Debí perder el conocimiento.*

bling *n.*

Se refiere a las joyas, normalmente muy ostentosas, que tanto gustan a los *rappers*.

bloke [UK] *n.*

TÍO, CHAVAL

—*Paul's a nice* **bloke**. • *Paul es un buen tío.*

a blonde moment *n.*

UN LAPSUS, UN MOMENTO DE ESTUPIDEZ

—*Sorry guys. I didn't mean to say*

that. I've just had **a blonde moment** • Perdonad, tíos, no quería decir eso. He tenido un lapsus.

blotto adj.
MUY PEDO, CIEGO/A
—You were **blotto** last night. • Ibas muy pedo anoche.

blow v., n.
1 CAGARLA
—Shit! You've **blown** it now. Shouldn't have done that! • ¡Mierda! La has cagado. ¡No deberías haberlo hecho!

2 FUNDIRSE (LA PASTA)
—I've **blown** all my dosh on this new mp4. • Me he fundido toda la pasta en este mp4.

3 CHUPÁRSELA A ALGUIEN (vul.)
—Oh, **blow** me baby! • ¡Vamos, chúpamela, cari!

4 [USA] FARLOPA, [UK] MARÍA
—Got any **blow**, mate? • ¿Tienes farlopa, tío?

blowjob n. (vul.)
MAMADA
—She gives good **blowjobs**. • La chupa bien.

blunder n.
CAGADA
—What a **blunder**! • ¡Qué cagada!

bo acron.
(body odour)
OLOR A TIGRE
—What's that ming? Somebody's got **bo**. • ¿Qué es ese pestazo? Alguien huele a tigre.

bob's your uncle expr.
AHÍ ESTÁ, YA ESTÁ, ESO ES
—Turn right, then second left and **bob's your uncle**. • Gira a la derecha, y coge la segunda a la izquierda, y ahí está.

bog down v.
ESTAR ESTANCADO/A, ESTAR BLOQUEADO/A
—We're getting **bogged down** with this. Let's move on. • Nos estamos estancando con esto. Sigamos con otra cosa.

bog standard [UK] adj.
DEL MONTÓN, NORMALUCHO
—They're a **bog standard** band. • Son un grupo del montón.

bollocking (give a) loc.
ECHAR UNA BRONCA
—She **gave me a** right **bollocking**. • Me echó una buena bronca.

bollocks [UK] n. pl.
1 COJONES, HUEVOS
—You don't have the **bollocks**, mate. • No tienes huevos, tío.

2 GILLIPOLLECES

—*You're talking **bollocks**.* • *Estás diciendo gilipolleces.*

3 ¡MIERDA!, ¡Y UNA MIERDA! *interj.*

—***Bollocks!** I'm gonna be late now!* • *¡Mierda! Ahora voy a llegar tarde.*

bomb *v.*

METERLE CAÑA, IR A TODA HOSTIA

—*That was quick! Did you **bomb** it?* • *¡Qué rápido! ¿Le has metido mucha caña, no?*

boner *n. (vul.)*

ESTAR EMPALMADO, ESTAR PALOTE

—*I've got a **boner**!* • *¡Estoy empalmado!*

bong *n.*

PIPA PARA FUMAR, CACHIMBA

—*Pass me the **bong**, man.* • *Pásame la pipa, tío.*

bonk *v. (vul.)*

ECHAR UN POLVO, FOLLAR

—*No **bonking** while I'm out.* • *Nada de folleteo mientras esté fuera.*

bonkers *adj.*

CHALADO/A, PIRADO/A

—*You're **bonkers**, mate!* • *¡Estás chalado, colega!*

booger, bogey *n.*

MOCO

—*Blow your nose, you pig. You've got **boogers**.* • *Suénate la nariz, cerdo, que la tienes llena de mocos.*

bookie's (the) *n.*

CASA DE APUESTAS, ENCARGADO/A DE LAS APUESTAS

—*Geezer 1: Going down the **bookie's**?* || *Geezer 2: No, mate. Got no dosh.* • *Tío 1:¿Vas a la casa de apuestas?* || *Tío 2: No, tío. No tengo pasta.*

booty, bootie *n.*

CULO, CULAZO, PANDERO

—*Oh, mama! What a **bootie**!* • *¡Joder! ¡Qué culazo!*

HAY MILES DE PALABRAS PARA DENOMINAR ESE LUGAR DONDE LA ESPALDA PIERDE SU ILUSTRE NOMBRE: ASS, ARSE, BACKYARD, BEHIND, BUM, BUTT, JACKSY, KEISTER, PATOOTIE, REAR END...

bootylicious *adj.*

QUE TIENE UN CUERPAZO

—Yeah, baby. Your so **bootylicious**. • ¡Vaya cuerpazo, tía!

booze *n.*

PRIVA, ALCOHOL

—No **booze**. You're driving. • Nada de priva. Tienes que conducir.

boozer *n.*

BAR, BARETO

—I'm off to the **boozer**. Coming? • Me voy al bareto. ¿Te apuntas?

bottle *n.*

COJONES, HUEVOS

—You ain't got the **bottle**, mate. • No tienes huevos, tío.

brick it *v.*

ESTAR CAGADO DE MIEDO

—I was **bricking it**! • ¡Estaba cagado de miedo!

bro' *abrev.*
(brother)

HERMANO, TRONCO, COLEGA

—Yo, **bro'**. Wassup? • ¿Qué pasa, tronco?

bum *v.*

DAR, PRESTAR

—**Bum** me a square, man. • Dame un piti, tío.

bummer *n.*

PUTADA

—Working on Saturdays? What a **bummer**! • ¿Curras los sábados? ¡Qué putada!

buns *n. pl.*

NALGAS

—That guy has nice **buns**. • Ese tío tiene unas buenas nalgas.

busted (get) *loc.*

PILLAR, DETENER

—Robert Downey Jr. **got busted** for heroin again! • ¡Han pillado otra vez a Robert Downey Jr. por posesión de heroína!

byob *acron.*
(bring your own beer)

TRAE BEBIDA

—Party at mine. Saturday. 9pm. **byob**. • Fiesta en mi casa. Sábado a las 9. Trae bebida.

STUART GOT CARDED AT THE CLUB LAST NIGHT// BUT HE'S 25!// YEAH BUT HE LOOKS 13 •A STUART LE PIDIERON EL CARNET AYER EN LA DISCO //¡PERO SI TIENE 25 AÑOS!// YA PERO APARENTA 13

de los 80, que decía **Don't cali-fornicate Oregon**. El término se ha puesto incluso más de moda gracias a la serie de TV *Californi-cation*, protagonizada por David "Mulder" Duchovny.

—*Californication is spreading!*
• *¡La "Californicación" está exten-diéndose!*

call it a day *expr.*
TERMINAR ALGO POR HOY

—*That's it! We're gonna **call it a day**.* • *¡Ya está! Por hoy, hemos acabado.*

cake *adj., n.*
1 FÁCIL, CHUPADO/A

—*This exercise is **cake**!* • *¡Este ejercicio está chupado!*

2 PASTA, GUITA

—*My kid's getting his **cake** this summer working in a beach bar.* • *Mi niño está ganando pasta este verano trabajando en un chiringuito.*

Californication *n.*
(California + fornication)

Hace referencia a las influencias de la forma de vida californiana en algunos estados occidentales de Estados Unidos; influencias ta-chadas por muchos de indecentes y lujuriosas. El término tiene su origen en una pegatina de coches aparecida en Oregon a principios

camp *adj.*
AFEMINADO, QUE TIENE PLUMA

—*That guy is so **camp**.* • *Ese tío tiene mucha pluma.*

candy *n.*
1 Eufemismo para "sexo" o "dro-gas". El término se usa mucho en el lenguaje callejero de las prosti-tutas y de los camellos.

—*Whore: Hey! You want some **candy**?* • *Puta: ¡Eh! ¿Quieres follar?*

—*Pusher: Hey! You want some **candy**?* • *Camello: ¡Eh! ¿Quieres pillar?*

2 ear candy *n.*
BUENA MÚSICA

—*That tune's **ear-candy**, man.* • *Eso es un temazo, tío.*

3 eye candy *n.*

UN REGALO PARA LA VISTA

—*Girlfriend: Stop eyeing up the birds. || Boyfriend: Don't worry baby. They're just **eye candy**. You're my true love.* • *Novia: Deja de comerte con la mirada a esas tías. || Novio: No te preocupes, cari, solo me alegro un poco la vista. Tú eres mi amor verdadero.*

4 nose candy *n.*

FARLOPA, RAYA

—*She needs her fix of **nose candy**.* • *Necesita su dosis de farlopa.*

card *v.*

Pedir el carnet a alguien que tiene aspecto joven, especialmente en la puerta de las discos.

—*Stuart got **carded** at the club last night. || But he's 25! || Yeah, but he looks 13.* • *A Stuart le pidieron el carnet ayer en la disco. || ¡Pero si tiene 25 años! || Ya, pero aparenta 13.*

chav [UK] *n.*

CHOLO/A, QUILLO/A

—*I'm not going back to that club. It's full of **chavs**.* • *No pienso volver a ese club. Está lleno de cholos.*

cheapskate *n.*

AGARRADO/A, RATA

—*Splash the cash, man! You're such a **cheapskate**!* • *¡Suelta la pasta, tío! ¡No seas tan agarrao!*

chedda [USA] *n.*

PASTA, GUITA

—*Hey man! You got the **chedda**?* • *¡Oye tío! ¿Tienes la pasta?*

chick *n.*

1 TÍA, CHURRI

—*I love Californian **chicks**.* • *Me encantan las tías de California.*

2 chick flick *n.*

UNA PELI PARA TÍAS

—*Don't go to see "The Sisterhood of the Travelling Pants"! It's a **chick flick**.* • *¡No vayas a ver "Uno para todas"! Es una peli para tías.*

chicken out *v.*

CAGARSE, ECHARSE ATRÁS

—*Girl: He didn't even say anything. He just **chickened out**.* • *Chica: No dijo ni mu. Se cagó.*

chief *n.*

JEFE, TÍO, COLEGA

—*Wassup, **chief**!* • *¡Qué pasa, tío!*

chill *v.*

1 QUEDARSE EN CASA EN PLAN TRANQUIS

—*I'm gonna **chill** with the guys tonight.* • *Voy a quedarme en casa de tranquis con los colegas esta noche.*

2 RELAJARSE

—***Chill**, man!* • *¡Relájate, colega!*

chillax v.
(chill + relax)
QUEDARSE EN CASA EN PLAN TRANQUIS

—*Come on over, we're just **chillaxin'** tonight.* • *Vente para acá, que vamos a quedarnos en casa en plan tranquis.*

chuck v.
1 TIRAR

—***Chuck** me the paper over, will you?* • *Tírame el periódico, por favor.*

2 MANDAR A PASEO, PLANTAR

—*Give me a beer. Martha's **chucked** me again.* • *Dame una birra, que Martha me ha vuelto a mandar a paseo.*

3 chuck up v.
POTAR

—*Lamar's flatmate: Are you OK, Lamar? //Lamar: No, man, I've just **chucked up**.* • *Compañero de piso de Lamar: ¿Estás bien, Lamar? //Lamar: No, tío, acabo de potar.*

chuff v.
TIRARSE UN PEDO

—*Oh, no! Who **chuffed**?* • *¡Joder!, ¿Quién se ha tirado un pedo?*

clam up loc. v.
QUEDARSE EN BLANCO

—*I didn't know what to say. I just **clammed up**.* • *No sabía que decir. Me quedé en blanco.*

clapped-out adj.
DESTARTALADO/A (COCHES O MÁQUINAS)

—*Are you still driving that **clapped-out** SEAT?* • *¿Todavía tienes aquel SEAT tan destartalado?*

cock n. (vul.)
1 POLLA

—*Knob down the disco: What you need is a good **cock**! // Girl: Piss off!* • *El típico capullo de discoteca: ¡Lo que necesitas es un buen pollón! // Chica: ¡Vete a la mierda!*

MUCHAS SON LAS PALABRAS USADAS PARA REFERIRSE A ESTE INSTRUMENTO: BOBBY, DICK, KNOB, PRICK, SAUSAGE, SCHLONG, TODGER, WANGER, WILLIE...

2 cockteaser n. (vul.)
CALIENTAPOLLAS, CALIENTABRAGUETAS

—*Watch out, Mary, your man is talking to that **cockteaser**!* • *¡Vigila, Mary, que tu novio está hablando con esa calientapollas!*

3 **cock up** *v.*

CAGARLA

—*Shit! I've **cocked** it **up** again.* •
¡Mierda! La he vuelto a cagar.

cold feet (get) *loc.*

PONERSE NERVIOSO/A Y
ECHARSE ATRÁS

—*Wilson: Did you ask her? // John-*
*son: No. // Wilson: Did you **get cold**
feet? // Johnson: Yeah.* • *Wilson: ¿Se*
lo pediste? // Johnson: No. // Wilson:
¿Te echaste atrás? // Johnson: Sí.

come, cum *v. (vul.)*

CORRERSE

—*Honey, I'm gonna **cum**!* • *¡Cari-*
ño, que me corro!

come out *v.*

SALIR DEL ARMARIO

—*Margaret **came out** to everyone*
after dinner. She has a steady girl-
friend now. • *Margaret salió del*
armario después de la cena. Ahora
tiene novia.

comptarded *adj.*
(computer + retarded)

NEGADO/A PARA LA
INFORMÁTICA

—*My parents are so **comptarded**.*
• *Mis padres son unos negados para*
la informática.

con *n., v.*

1 ESTAFA, PUFO

—*This is a **con**.* • *Vaya pufo.*

2 JUGÁRSELA A ALGUIEN

—*Don't try to **con** me.* • *No inten-*
tes jugármela.

condomonium *n.*

NO TENER CONDONES A MANO

—*Yeah, we were just ready to get it*
*on and suddenly it was **condomo-***
***nium**.* • *Estábamos a punto de*
hacerlo y de repente nos dimos
cuenta de que no teníamos condones.

cool *adj.*

GUAY

—*Your bike's so **cool**.* • *Me mola*
mucho tu moto.

cough up *v.*

SOLTAR LA PASTA, AFLOJAR

—*Come on, dad. **Cough up**!* •
Venga, papi. ¡Suelta la pasta!

cow *n.*

CHICA CON MALA LECHE

—*She's such a **cow**!* • *¡Tiene*
muy mala leche!

crack up *v.*

1 PARTIRSE EL CULO DE RISA

—*Laugh? I was **cracking up**!* •
¿Que si me reí? ¡Me partí el culo!

2 DARLE ALGO

—Don't do that or dad'll **crack up**.
• No hagas eso o a papá le dará algo.

crap n., adj.

1 CACA, TRUÑO

—I'm going for a **crap**. • Voy a
echar un truño.

2 UNA MIERDA

—The flick was **crap**. • La peli era
una mierda.

crash v.

IRSE A LA PILTRA, IRSE AL
SOBRE

—I've had enough. I'm gonna
crash. • Ya no puedo más. Me voy
a la piltra.

cred n.

Nivel de respeto, prestigio o
credibilidad en el barrio. Se suele
usar en la expresión **street cred**.

—Don't wear that, you'll lose your
street **cred**. • No lleves eso; perderás
todo tu prestigio.

creep n.

CAPULLO, JETA, TIPARRACO

—He did what? Oh, man, he's
such a **creep**. Forget him. • ¿Que
hizo qué? ¡Joder, vaya capullo!
Olvídate de él.

crs acron.
(can't remember shit)

NO RECUERDO UNA MIERDA

—sms 1:WTF happened? ||sms 2:
crs. • sms 1: ¿Qué coño pasó? ||
sms 2: No recuerdo una mierda.

cut one v.

TIRARSE UN PEDO

—What's that smell? Who **cut one**?
• ¿Y ese olor? ¿Quién se ha tirado
un pedo?

cyberdump v.

PLANTAR A ALGUIEN POR
E-MAIL O POR MESSENGER

—Salvatore didn't have the balls to
say it to my face. He **cyberdumped**
me. • Salvatore no tuvo los huevos
de decírmelo a la cara y me plantó
por messenger.

cybersex n.

SEXO VIRTUAL

—Dawson: Have you ever tried
cybersex? ||Margaret: No, that's
for perverts. Have you? ||Dawson:
Erm... No, no, of course not. •
Dawson: ¿Has probado ya el sexo
virtual? ||Margaret: No, eso es de
pervertidos. ¿Y tú? ||Dawson: Eh...
No, no, claro que no.

MAN, THIS DICTIONARY'S THE DOG'S BOLLOCKS •
JODER, ESTE DICCIONARIO ES LA LECHE

d-boy _n._
CAMELLO

—Right, **d-boy**. You're nicked! •
¡Eh, tú, camello! ¡Estás detenido!

damage _n._
LA CUENTA, LA DOLOROSA

—Customer: What's the **damage**?
// Barman: $45. // Customer: What?
That's a rip-off! • Cliente: ¿Cuánto
es la dolorosa? // Camarero: 45$. //
Cliente: ¿Qué? ¡Vaya estafa!

dead _adv._
SUPER, MOGOLLÓN DE,
MAZO DE

—This is **dead** easy. • Esto es
superfácil.

dead beat _adj._
HECHO/A POLVO, DESTROZADO/A

—I'm gonna crash. I'm **dead beat**.
• Me voy a la piltra. Estoy hecho
polvo.

deck _v._
PEGAR UNA HOSTIA, PARTIRLE
LA CARA A ALGUIEN

—I'm gonna **deck** you! • ¡Te voy a
pegar una hostia!

decks _n._
PLATOS (DE UN DJ)

—And, on the **decks** tonite…
DJ Flash! • Y en los platos esta
noche… ¡DJ Flash!

deep-six _v._
1 DESHACERSE DE ALGUIEN,
CARGARSE A ALGUIEN

—He **deep-sixed** him. He's pus-
hing up daisies now. • Se lo cargó.
Ahora está criando malvas.

2 give something the deep-six
TIRAR, DESHACERSE DE ALGO

—Give that shit the **deep-six**! •
¡Tira toda esa mierda!

deep shit (to be in) _loc._
ESTAR DE MIERDA HASTA EL
CUELLO, ESTAR JODIDO/A

—Johnson, your **in deep shit** now.
• Johnson, ahora sí que estás jodido.

def *adj.*

COJONUDO/A, DE PUTA MADRE

—*That's a **def** bike.* • *Esa moto es cojonuda.*

deface *v.*

BORRAR A ALGUIEN DEL FACEBOOK

—*I **defaced** him. He was a creep anyway.* • *Lo borré de mi facebook. Total, era un capullo.*

dick *n. (vul.)*

1 POLLA

—*I've got a big **dick**.* • *Tengo un buen pollón.*

2 GILIPOLLAS

—*He's such a **dick**!* • *¡Es un gilipollas!*

OTRAS PALABRAS PARECIDAS: DICKHEAD, DIPSTICK, DIV, DIVVY, ETC.

3 dick around *v.*

HACER EL GILIPOLLAS

—*Linus, stop **dicking around**. I need it "by this afternoon".* • *Linus, deja de hacer el gilipollas, lo necesito para esta tarde.*

dig *v.*

MOLAR, FLIPAR, CHIFLAR

—*I really **dig** your music, man.* • *Me mola mazo tu música, tío.*

ding *interj.*

Especie de grito de victoria en los juegos de internet al llegar a un nivel nuevo.

—*sms 1: **ding!** || sms 2: Wot level? || sms 1: 16 || sms 2: omg* • *sms 1: ¡He llegado a un nivel nuevo! || sms 2: ¿Cuál? || sms 1: 16 || sms 2: ¡Joder!*

ding-dong [UK] *n.*

PELEA, BRONCA, JALEO

—*There was a right **ding-dong** down the pub last night.* • *Hubo mucho jaleo anoche en el pub.*

dinks *acron.*

(double income no kids)

Término con el que se designa a parejas que comparten el mismo techo, traen dos sueldos a casa y no tienen hijos.

dirty *adj.*

CACHONDO/A, CALIENTE, MORBOSO/A, VERDE, PORNO

1 dirty weekend

FINDE SEXUAL

2 dirty movie

PELI PORNO

3 dirty old man

VIEJO VERDE

También actúa como enfatizador de algunos adjetivos, especialmente los de tamaño.

—*There was this **dirty** big hole.* • *Había un pedazo de agujero.*

dish [UK] *n.*
TÍO/A BUENO/A

—*Have you seen the bloke in marketing? He's such a **dish**.* • *¿Has visto al tío de marketing? ¡Está buenísimo!*

ditch *v.*
PLANTAR A ALGUIEN, DESHACERSE DE ALGO

—*You really should **ditch** that creep!* • *¡A ese gilipollas deberías plantarle!*

dive [UK] *n.*
CUCHITRIL, ANTRO

—*This place is a **dive**.* • *Este sitio es un cuchitril.*

do *v.*
Es un verbo multiuso. Aquí tienes algunos de sus usos informales más frecuentes.

—*You've been **done**, mate.* • *Tío, te han timado.*

—*I don't **do** hard drugs.* • *Paso de drogas duras.*

—*He **does** something for me.* • *Me pone cachonda.*

—*She **does** my head in.* • *Me toca los huevos.*

doddle [UK] *n.*
PAN COMIDO

—*This is a **doddle**!* • *¡Esto es pan comido!*

dodgy *adj.*
CHUNGO/A

—*Let's go! This place is **dodgy**.* • *¡Vámonos de aquí! Este sitio es muy chungo.*

dog *n.*
CALLO, CARDO

—*Mary's a **dog**.* • *Mary es un callo.*

the dog's bollocks [UK] *loc.*
LA LECHE, LA HOSTIA, LO MÁS

—*Man, this dictionary's **the dog's bollocks**.* • *Joder, este diccionario es la leche.*

dole (on the) *loc.*
SIN CURRO, EN EL PARO

—*I've been **on the dole** for 8 years now.* • *Llevo 8 años en el paro.*

dope *n.*
1 IDIOTA

—*You **dope**! You've ballsed it up again.* • *¡Idiota! La has cagado otra vez.*

2 MARÍA, HIERBA

—*He just sits there smoking **dope** all day.* • *Se pasa el día ahí sentado fumando maría.*

dork [USA] *n., adj.*

CAPULLO

—*You're such a **dork**!* • *¡Qué capullo eres!*

dosh [UK] *n.*

PASTA, GUITA, MONI

—*Got any **dosh**?* • *¿Tienes pasta?*

doss *v.*

1 SOBAR EN CASA DE ALGUIEN

—*I'm **dossing** at Kyle's place 2nite.* • *Hoy sobo en casa de Kyle.*

2 doss around *v.*

NO HACER NADA EN PARTICULAR

—*What did you do in Paris? // We just **dossed around**.* • *¿Qué hicisteis en París? // Nada en particular.*

dosser *n., adj.*

PRINGADO/A, INÚTIL

—*He's a right **dosser*** • *Es muy pringao.*

dot-com millionaire *n.*

MILLONARIO PUNTO COM

Término que se usa para referirse a personas que se han hecho millonarias a través de internet. Un claro ejemplo es Mark Zuckerberg, fundador de facebook.

dot-gone *n.*

A **dot-gone** es una empresa de internet que no ha tenido éxito, que no se ha comido una rosca en el mundo del **e-business**.

—*He lost it all in that **dot-gone**.* • *Lo perdió todo en ese fiasco de empresa de internet.*

dough [USA] *n.*

PASTA, GUITA, MONI

—*You got any **dough**?* • *¿Tienes pasta?*

down low *adj.*

TOP SECRET

—*OK, dude! It's **down low**!* • *Vale, tío. ¡Top secret!*

downsize *v.*

REDUCIR LA PLANTILLA

—*Right, everbody! Listen up. They're **downsizing** the company.* • *¡Atención todo el mundo! Escuchad. Van a reducir la plantilla.*

drama queen *n.*

TEATRERO/A

—*Don't be such a **drama queen**.* • *No seas tan teatrera.*

drop _v._

1 PARTIRLE LA CARA A ALGUIEN

—If he says one more thing, I'm gonna **drop** him! • Si vuelve a abrir la boca, le parto los morros.

2 GASTAR, FUNDIRSE LA PASTA

—She **dropped** big dollar on that bling. • Se gastó un pastón en esas joyas.

3 METERSE (ESPECIALMENTE PASTILLAS)

—She **dropped** an E at the party. • Se metió un éxtasis en la fiesta.

drop a sprog _loc._

PARIR

—I see Tina's **dropped** another **sprog**. • Veo que Tina ha vuelto a parir.

drop dead gorgeous _adj._

GUAPÍSIMA/O, BUENÍSIMA/O

—Oh man! Look at that dudette. She's **drop dead gorgeous**. • ¡Tío! Mira a esa pava. ¡Está buenísima!

drop it _expr._

DÉJALO

dude [USA] _n._

TÍO, COLEGA, TRONCO

—Wassup, **dude**! • ¿Qué pasa, tío?

dudette [USA] _n._

TÍA, COLEGA, TRONCA

—**Dudette**! Your so cool! • ¡Tia, eres lo más!

duff _adj._

1 LO PEOR, MALÍSIMO/A

—I'm not coming back to another game. We're so **duff**. • No vuelvo a otro partido. ¡Somos lo peor!

2 up the duff [UK] _adj._

EMBARAZADA, PREÑADA

—I see her from next door is **up the duff** again. • Veo que la vecina está otra vez preñada.

dump _n._

1 CUCHITRIL, ANTRO

—This place is a **dump**. • Este sitio es un cuchitril.

2 take a dump _loc. (vul.)_

CAGAR, PLANTAR UN PINO

—David's gone to **take a dump**. • David se ha ido a cagar.

3 dump someone _v._

DEJAR A ALGUIEN, PLANTAR

—Give me a beer. Martha's **dumped** me again. • Dame una birra, Marta me ha vuelto a dejar.

3 dump on someone _v._

PONER VERDE A ALGUIEN

—Quit **dumping** on me you asshole! • ¡Deja de ponerme verde, capullo!

e *n.*
ÉXTASIS

—*Jay: How are you mate?* || *Jim: I'm benevolent. I feel like a big, fat Buddha!* || *Jay: Have you dropped an **e**, mate?* • *Jay:¿Cómo estás tío?* || *Jim: ¡Me siento tan compasivo como un Buda enorme!* || *Jay: ¿Te has metido un éxtasis, o qué?*

e- *prefijo*
1 e-dress *n.*
DIRECCIÓN DE MAIL O DE WEB

2 e-famous *n.*
ALGUIEN QUE PRESUME DE SER FAMOSO EN INTERNET

3 e-gret *n., v.*
LAMENTAR ALGO QUE HAS HECHO EN INTERNET

—*I **e-gret** the day I gave you my e-dress.* • *Maldigo el día que te di mi e-mail.*

4 e-loan *n.*
PRÉSTAMO EN LINEA

5 e-love *n.*
AMOR VIRTUAL

6 e-tail *n.*
"SHOPPING" EN LÍNEA

7 e-zine *n.*
REVISTA QUE SE ENCUENTRA SOLO EN INTERNET

ear worm *n.*
CANCIÓN O MELODÍA ODIOSA QUE SE ENGANCHA

—*I've got an **ear worm** now. I hate the Birdy Song.* • *Se me ha enganchado la maldita canción de los pajaritos.*

easy-peasy *adj.*
CHUPADO/A

—*Don't worry, guys. This is **easy-peasy**.* • *No os preocupéis. Esto está chupado.*

eat it, eat shit *expr.*
TOMA YA, CHÚPATE ESA, CÓMETE ESA

—*Yes! **Eat it!** 3-0!* • *¡Sí! ¡Toma ya! ¡3 a 0!*
—*UV been owned. **Eat shit!*** • *Te he machacado. ¡Chúpate esa!*

edge city *loc.*
HISTÉRICO/A

—*Don't go in there, man. She's in* **edge city** *this morning.* • *No entres ahí, tío. Está histérica esta mañana.*

edge it *expr.*
CUIDADO, AL LORO

—**Edge it!** *The pigs are here!* • *¡Cuidado! ¡La pasma!*

effing *adj., adv.*
PUTO/A

—*The* **effing** *car won't start* • *El puto coche no arranca.*

eff off *expr.*
QUE TE JODAN

egg on *v.*
ANIMAR, INCITAR

—*We were* **egging** *him* **on.** *So, he went and did it.* • *Estuvimos animándolo, así que fue y lo hizo.*

elbow bending *n.*
1 EMPINAR EL CODO

—*Sophie: What are you doing tonight, then?* || *Roger: A bit of* **elbow bending** *down the "Dog and Duck".* • *Sophie: ¿Qué haces esta noche?* || *Roger: Empinaremos un poco el codo en el "Dog and Duck".*

2 give someone the elbow *loc.*
MANDAR A PASEO, CORTAR CON ALGUIEN

—*He's a creep. Why don't you just* **give** *him* **the elbow**? • *Es un capullo. ¿Por qué no lo mandas a paseo de una vez?*

emo *n.*
Subcultura que surgió a mediados de los 80 como un género musical que, debido al contenido emocional, fue definido como *emotional hardcore*, y posteriormente abreviado como *emo-core*. Los *emo* mantienen una actitud crítica con la sociedad centrada en las emociones: dolor, rabia, desgracia, insatisfacción, etc.

end
1 things your end *loc.*
TU VIDA, TUS COSAS, TÚ MISMO/A

—*How are* **things your end**? • *¿Cómo te van las cosas?*

2 get your end away *v.*
ECHAR UN POLVO, FOLLAR

—**Get your end away** *at the weekend?* • *¿Follaste el finde?*

eye up *v.*
ECHAR EL OJO A ALGUIEN, COMER CON LOS OJOS

—*Look at that hunk. He's* **eyeing** *you* **up.** • *Mira al buenorro ese. Te está comiendo con la mirada.*

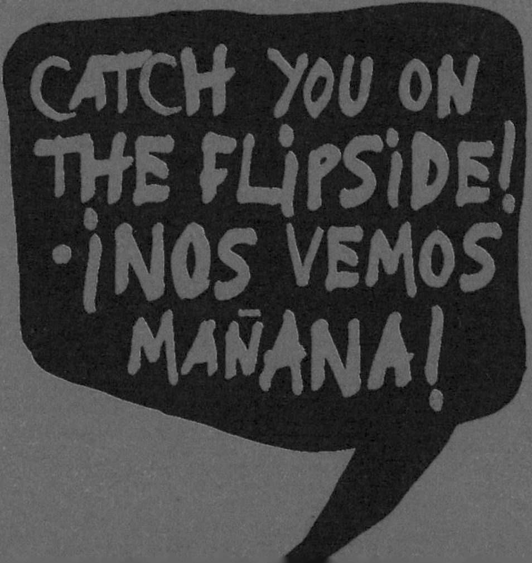
CATCH YOU ON THE FLIPSIDE!
¡NOS VEMOS MAÑANA!

faboo *abrev.*
(fabulous)
GENIAL

—*Messenger 1: Ding! Level 16.* // *Messenger 2: Faboo!* • *Messenger 1: ¡He llegado al nivel 16!* // *Messenger 2: ¡Genial!*

face time *n.*
CARA A CARA

—*Listen, honey. Come on over. We need some face time.* • *Oye, cariño, vente pa' cá que tenemos que hablar cara a cara.*

faff around/about *v.*
HACER EL CHORRA

—*Stop faffing around!* • *¡Deja de hacer el chorra!*

fag *n.*
1 [UK] PITILLO, CIGARRILLO

—*Got a fag, mate?* • *¿Tienes un pitillo?*

2 [USA] MARICÓN *(vul.)*

—*Are you a fag?* • *¿Eres maricón?*

fair-doos *interj.*
VALE, NO PASA NADA

—*I'll be a bit late.* // *OK, fair-doos.* • *Llegaré un poco tarde.* // *Ok, no pasa nada.*

fake bake *n.*
MORENO (DE) UVA

—*Woman: She's so tacky! Check the fake bake.* • *Mujer: ¡Qué cutre la tía con este moreno uva que lleva!*

fall on the grenade *loc.*
LIGAR CON LA FEA PARA QUE TU AMIGO CONSIGA LA GUAPA

—*OK, man. I'm going for that blonde; the good looking one. It's your turn to fall on the grenade.* • *Vale. Yo voy a por la rubia, la guapa. A ti te toca la fea esta vez.*

family jewels *n.*
PELOTAS, HUEVOS

—*Footballer: Careful with the family jewels, man! It's the big ball you're meant to kick.* • *Futbolista: ¡Oye, cuidado con mis pelotas! Es la pelota grande a la que tienes que darle.*

fanny *n.*

1 [UK] CHOCHO, POTORRO *(vul.)*

—Knob down the disco: Show me your *fanny*, baby! || Girl: Piss off! • El típico capullo de discoteca: ¡Enséñame el chocho, guapa! || Chica: ¡Vete a la mierda!

2 [USA] CULO

—Move your *fanny*! • ¡Mueve el culo!

faqs *acron.*
(frequently asked questions)
PREGUNTAS FRECUENTES

far out *adj.*
INCREÍBLE, FLIPANTE

—Like, this is so *far out*, man. • Buah, tío, esto es increíble.

fart *n., v.*
1 PEDO

—A *fart* can ruin your life. • Un pedo te puede arruinar la vida.

2 TIRARSE UN PEDO

—Who *farted*? • ¿Quién se ha tirado un pedo?

3 farting terms *n.*
Fase a la que llega una pareja cuando el grado de intimidad es tan alto que la relación no se ve afectada por el intercambio de flatulencias.

—How's your relationship going? || Great! We're on *farting terms* now. • ¿Cómo va vuestra relación? || ¡Fenomenal! Ya nos tiramos pedos sin pudor.

4 brain fart *n.*
BLOQUEO, EMPANADA MENTAL

—I had a total *brain fart* when he asked me that question. • Me quedé totalmente bloqueado cuando me hizo esa pregunta.

fatty *n.*
PORRO GIGANTE, PORRACO

—Nice! A big *fatty*! • ¡Joder! ¡Vaya porraco!

feel up *v.*
METER MANO, MANOSEAR

—What's wrong? || That prick just *felt* me *up*! • ¿Qué te pasa? || ¡Ese gilipollas acaba de meterme mano!

feel it *v.*
FLIPAR, MOLAR

—Oh, man! I *feel it*, I *feel it*! • ¡Joder, tío! ¡Me mola, me mola!

2 feel it hard *expr.*
TOMA YA

—I own U. *Feel it hard*! • Te he ganado. ¡Toma ya!

fell off the back of a lorry [UK] *expr.*

MANGAR, ROBAR

—*Where did you get that new flat screen TV?* || *It **fell off the back of a lorry**, mate.* • *¿De dónde has sacado esta tele de plasma?* || *La mangué, tío.*

-fiend

Sufijo que se añade a un nombre y que indica que uno/a es fanático/a de esa cosa.

—*She's a Star Wars-**fiend**.* • *Es fanática de la Guerra de las Galaxias.*

filthy rich *adj.*

ASQUEROSAMENTE RICO/A

—*Rich? He's **filthy rich**!* • *¿Rico? ¡Es asquerosamente rico!*

fink on/out *v.*

JUGÁRSELA A ALGUIEN, PEGÁRSELA A ALGUIEN

—*Johnson: Right, who **finked** me **out**?* || *Wilson: I dunno!* • *Johnson: A ver, ¿quién me la ha jugado?* || *Wilson: ¡No sé!*

first base *n.*

MORREO, BESUQUEO

—*Dennis: Did you get any action at the weekend?* || *Chris: Not much. I just got to **first base**.* • *Dennis: ¿Mojaste este finde?* || *Chris: No, solo unos morreos.*

fish market *n.*

MUCHAS MUJERES JUNTAS, GALLINERO

—*It's like a **fish market** in here. Is that a hen party?* • *¡Cuánta mujer suelta! ¿Hay una despedida de soltera, o qué?*

fit *adj.*

SEXY, CAÑÓN, TÍO/A BUENO/A

—*Have you seen that new bird in accounts? She's **fit**!* • *¿Has visto a la tía nueva de contabilidad? ¡Está cañón!*

fives *expr.*

Esta expresión se usa normalmente para expresar la posesión de algo.

—*Anyone for the last beer?* || ***Fives** on that!* • *¿Alguien quiere la última birra?* || *¡Para mí!*

fix *n.*

1 DOSIS

No solo se usa con drogas sino con cualquier cosa a la que estás enganchado/a.

—*I need my **fix** of PS3.* • *Necesito mi dosis de PS3.*

2 MONTAJE

—*Their relationship's a **fix**.* • *Su relación es un montaje.*

flash v., n.

1 ENSEÑAR LOS ATRIBUTOS EN PÚBLICO

—*Everybody: Sparky, **flash** your arse! // Sparky: Okey-dokey. •*
Todos: Sparky, ¡bájate los pantalones! // Sparky: Vale.

2 FANTASMA, CHULO/A

—*Jealous man 1: Look at him in his new car. // Jealous man 2: **Flash** git! • Envidioso 1: Míralo con su coche nuevo. // Envidioso 2: ¡Vaya fantasma!*

flexitarian n.
(flexible + vegetarian)

Vegetariano/a "light" que en ciertas ocasiones no tiene problemas en comer huevos, productos lácteos, pescado o incluso carne.

—*Wanna a tuna and bacon omelette? // Yeah, man! I'm a **flexitarian**!*
• *¿Quieres una tortilla de atún y bacon?// ¡Sí, venga! ¡Soy "flexitariano"!*

flicks (the) [UK] n.

CINE, PELI

—*What's on at **the flicks**, mate? // Nothing, just chick flicks. • ¿Qué ponen en el cine? // Nada, solo pelis para tías.*

fling n.

LÍO, ROLLO

—*Piss head: Well, I was having a **fling** with that bird from accounts.*
So, Martha found out. And, well she dumped me. // Barman: Are you talking to me? • Borrachuzo: Bueno, tenía un rollo con una tía de contabilidad. Entonces, se enteró Marta. Y, bueno, me dejó. // Camarero: ¿Estás hablando conmigo

flip v.

CABREARSE, VOLVERSE LOCO/A

—*Piss head: Well, Martha **flipped** when she found out. // Barman: Here, get this down you. • Borrachuzo: Bueno, pues, Marta se cabreó cuando se dio cuenta. // Camarero: venga, tómate esto.*

flipside (on the)

[USA] *loc. adv.*

MAÑANA

—*Catch you **on the flipside**. • Nos vemos mañana.*

floor v.

1 DAR UNA HOSTIA

—*I'm gonna **floor** you! • ¡Te voy a dar una hostia!*

2 QUEDARSE HECHO/A POLVO

—*I was **floored** by the devastating news. • Me quedé hecha polvo cuando me enteré de la noticia.*

floss [USA] v.

FARDAR, FANTASMEAR

—*Once he got the new car, he couldn't help but **floss**. • Desde que se compró el coche, no paraba de fardar.*

flow [USA] *n.*

1 GRACIA Y DESTREZA A LA HORA DE RAPEAR

—*Kanye West got the* **flow***!* • *¡Kanye West rapea de puta madre!*

2 PASTA, GUITA

—*Show me the* **flow***.* • *Enséñame la pasta.*

3 go with the flow *loc.*
HACER LO QUE DECIDAN LOS DEMÁS, SEGUIR LA CORRIENTE

—*Bird from accounts: What do you wanna do? || Johnson: I dunno. I'll just* **go with the flow***.* • *Tía de contabilidad: ¿Qué quieres hacer? || Johnson: No sé. Lo que queráis.*

flunk *v.*
CATEAR

—*Shit! I've* **flunked** *all my exams.* • *¡Mierda! He cateado todos los exámenes.*

flush [UK] *adj.*
FORRADO/A

—*The drinks are on him! He's* **flush***.* • *¡Las copas las paga él! Que está forrao.*

fly *adj.*
Dependiendo del lado del charco en el que estés tiene un significado u otro; en Estados Unidos significa "guay", pero en Gran Bretaña es "chungo/a".

1 [USA]

—*Brian's a* **fly** *man.* • *Brian es un tío guay.*

2 [UK]

—*He's a* **fly** *man. He waltzed off with my drink.* • *¡Qué chungo el tío! Me ha mangado la copa.*

fob off *v.*
CAMELAR, EMBAUCAR, TIMAR

—*He* **fobbed** *me* **off** *with a lame excuse.* • *Me ha camelado con una excusa patética.*

food coma *n.*
MODORRA QUE TE ENTRA DESPUÉS DE COMER MUCHO

—*We all fell into a* **food coma** *after lunch.* • *A todos nos entró la modorra después de comer.*

foodie *n.*
COCINITAS

—*No! No garlic! Everybody knows that! || You're such a* **foodie***.* • *¡No! ¡No pongas ajo! ¡Cómo se te ocurre! || Tío, eres un cocinitas.*

fork out *v.*
AFLOJAR, SOLTAR PASTA

—*I had to* **fork out** *$1000 for the ring.* • *Tuve que aflojar 1000 dólares por el anillo.*

frag _v._

LIQUIDAR
Término muy utilizado en los
juegos de ordenador.

—I **fragged** you! lol. • ¡Te he liquidado! Ja ja ja.

freak _n._

FÁNATICO/A, FRIQUI
—He's a music-**freak**. • Es un
fanático de la música.

freak out _v._

1 FLIPAR EN COLORES
—I **freaked out** when I heard my
ex was preggers. • Flipé en colores
cuando me enteré de que mi ex estaba preñada.

2 ACOJONARSE, CAGARSE
—Let's get out of this dodgy place.
It's **freaking** me **out**. • Salgamos
de este antro tan chungo que me
estoy acojonando.

freeballin' _v._

IR SIN GAYUMBOS
—Hey, Jock! Like the kilt! Are you
freeballin'? • ¡Oye, Jock! ¡Me gusta
tu falda! ¿Vas sin gayumbos?

fresh _adj._

CHULO/A, GUAPO/A
—Look at my new wheels. // **Fresh**,
man. Fresh. • Mira mi nuevo buga.
// Guapo, tío, muy guapo.

friend with benefits _n._

AMIGO/A CON DERECHO A ROCE
—Are you two an item? // No,
we're just **friends with benefits**. •
¿Sois novios? // No, solo amigos con
derecho a roce.

front _n._

TAPADERA
—The fuzz: Right, admit it! The
casino's just a **front**, innit? • La
pasma: ¡Venga, admítelo! El casino es
una tapadera, ¿verdad?

frottage _n._

MAGREO, SOBETEO
—Wilson: Did you get past first
base? // Johnson: Yeah, man. A bit of
frottage. • Wilson: ¿Hubo algo más
que besos? // Johnson: Sí, tío. Un poco
de magreo.

frumpy _adj._

CALLO, CARDO
—If she just made an effort, she
wouldn't be so **frumpy**. • Con que
se arreglara un poquito, no parecería
tan callo.

ftw _acron._
(for the win)

Utilizado en juegos de internet u
ordenador.

A POR TODAS, A GANAR

fud *acron.*
(fear uncertainty doubt)
CAMPAÑA DE DESPRESTIGIO

—*That software's OK. Don't believe the **fud**.* • *Ese software está bien. No te creas la campaña de desprestigio.*

fugly *adj.*
(fucking ugly)
FEÍSIMO/A

—*Have you seen that other bird in accounts?* || *Yeah, man. **Fugly**!* • *¿Has visto a la otra chica de contabilidad?* || *Sí, tío, feísima.*

fularious *adj.*
(fucking hilarious)
FLIPANTE, COJONUDO/A

—*Oh, man! That's **fularious**!* • *¡Tío, eso es flipante!*

full monty *n.*
UN COMPLETO

—*Landlady: Do you want an English breakfast?* || *Guest: Yes, please. I'll have the **full monty**.* • *Patrona: ¿Quiere el desayuno inglés?* || *Invitado: Sí, por favor, un completo.*

fun police *n.*
AGUAFIESTAS

Existen muchas expresiones compuestas con el término **police** que sirven para designar a personas que intentan controlarlo todo. Por ejemplo, **the fun police**, **the music police**, etc.

—*Hey! Get that music off! It sucks ass!* || *The **music police** have arrived!* • *¡Oye! ¡Quita esa música! ¡Es una mierda!* || *Ya ha llegado el plasta de la música.*

—*Think your funny?* || *Oops, the **fun police** are here too.* • *¿Te crees muy gracioso?* || *Uf, ya está aquí el aguafiestas.*

funk button *n.*
BOTÓN IMAGINARIO QUE ACTIVA LA EUFORIA O LA PASIÓN

—*That pushed my **funk button**.* • *Eso me pone mucho.*

fuzz (the) *n.*
LA POLI, LA PASMA

—*The **fuzz** are here.* • *Ha llegado la pasma.*

fuzzbuster *n.*
DETECTOR DE RADAR

—*Wilson: Slow down, man!* || *Johnson: It's Ok. I've got a **fuzzbuster** fitted.* • *Wilson: ¡Ve más despacio, tío!* || *Johnson: No te preocupes, que llevo detector de radar.*

fuzzy math(s) *n.*
ALGO DEMASIADO COMPLEJO Y CONFUSO

—*Dave: Got that?* || *Pete: No. It's **fuzzy math** to me.* • *Dave: ¿Me entiendes?* || *Pete: No. Esto es demasiado complicao para mí.*

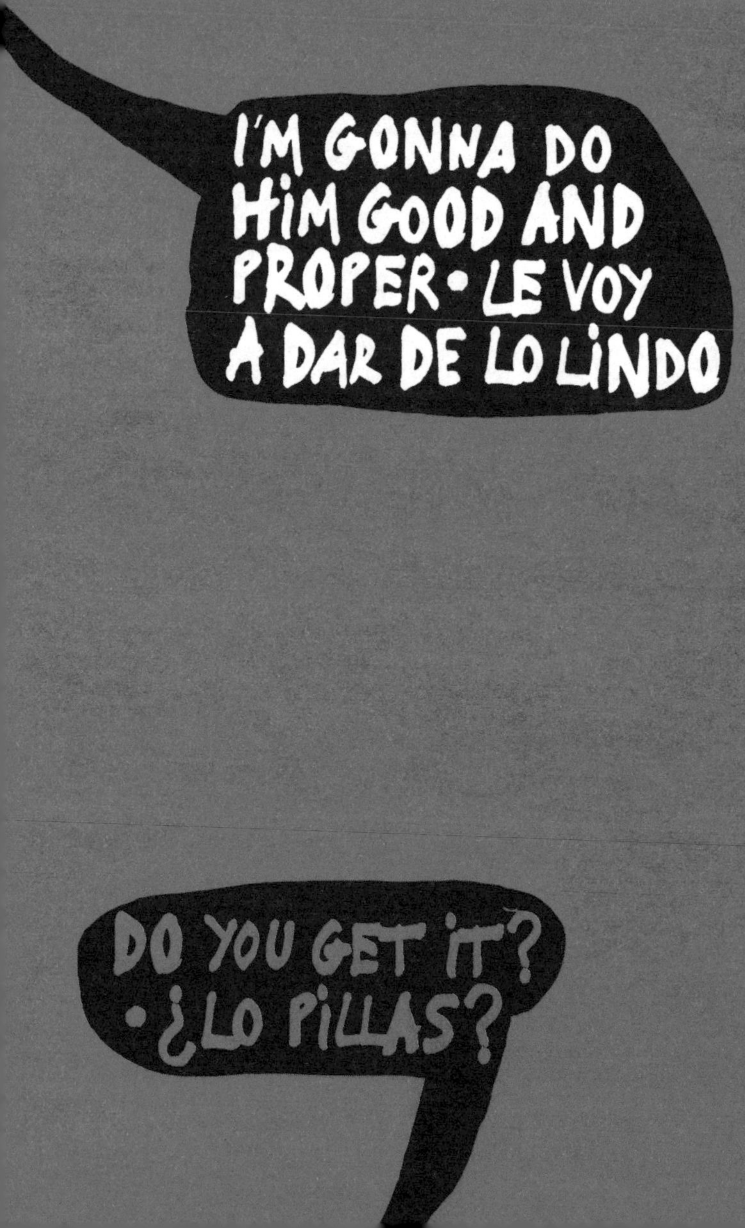
I'M GONNA DO HIM GOOD AND PROPER • LE VOY A DAR DE LO LINDO
DO YOU GET IT? • ¿LO PILLAS?

g2g *acron.*
(got to go)
TENGO QUE IRME
Expresión muy usada en chats.

gag for *v.*
MORIRSE DE GANAS

—I'm **gagging** for a fag. •
Me muero de ganas de fumarme
un piti.

game (be) *loc.*
APUNTARSE, TENER GANAS

—Bird from accounts: Anybody
fancy a pint after work? || Johnson:
I'm game. • Tía de contabilidad:
¿A alguien le hace una birra después
del curro? || Johnson: Yo me apunto.

game over *expr.*
SE ACABÓ, FINITO, Y ADIÓS
MUY BUENAS

—Piss head: So, Martha found
out and it was **game over**. •
Borrachuzo: Total, que Martha se
enteró y se acabó.

gammy [UK] *adj.*
CHUNGO/A

—I can't play tonight. I've got a
gammy leg. • Hoy no puedo jugar.
Tengo la pierna chunga.

ganja *n.*
MARÍA, HIERBA

—Got any **ganja** for my bong? •
¿Tienes hierba para mi arguila?

gank [USA] *v.*
CHORIZAR, MANGAR

—Chas: Where did you get that,
then? || Dave: I **ganked** it. •
Chas: Entonces, ¿de dónde lo has
sacado? || Dave: Lo mangué.

gatecrash *v.*
COLARSE

—Donald: How did you manage
to get an invite? || Scoop: I didn't.
I just **gatecrashed**. • Donald: ¿Có-
mo conseguiste una invita? || Scoop:
No, si no tenía invita. Me colé.

gear *n.*

BÁRTULOS, EQUIPO, TRASTOS

—*Have you seen my fishing **gear**?* •
¿Has visto mis bártulos de pesca?

geek *n.*

FRIQUI, COLGADO/A

—*Mike: Going out tonight? // Ted:
No, I can't, man. I'm playing World
Conquest on facebook tonight. //
Friend: **Geek**!* • *Mike: ¿Sales hoy?
// Ted: No puedo, tío, tengo una parti-
da de World Conquest en facebook.//
Mike: ¡Qué friqui!*

geezer [UK] *n.*

1 TÍO, CHAVAL, TIPO

—*Roger: Who's that **geezer** at the
bar? // Kieran: That's Martha's ex.*
• *Roger: ¿Quién es ese tipo de la barra? // Kieran: Es el ex de Marta.*

2 diamond geezer [UK] *n.*

TÍO COJONUDO

—*You're a **diamond geezer**, mate!*
• *¡Eres un tío cojonudo!*

LONDINENSE DE PURA CEPA

—*What Dave? The **diamond geezer**?* • *¿Qué Dave? ¿El londinense?*

3 geezer bird [UK] *n.*

MARIMACHO

—*Kieran: Who's that bloke at the
bar talking to Martha's ex? //
Roger: That's not a bloke, it's a bird.
// Kieran: No way! A **geezer bird**
more like.* • *Kieran: ¿Quién es ese*
tío de la barra que está hablando
con el ex de Marta? // No es un tío,
es una tía.// ¡No jodas! ¡Pues vaya
marimacho!

gel *v.*

CONGENIAR, PEGAR

—*Ok, we're going out for a fag. We'll
let those two guys **gel**.* • *Vale, salgamos a fumar un piti, así les dejamos
a ver si congenian.*

get a grip *expr.*

TRANQUI, CONTRÓLATE,
CÁLMATE

—*Hey man! **Get a grip**, will you?* •
¡Oye tio! Tranqui, ¿eh?

get a life *expr.*

ESTÁS COLGADO/A

—*Boy: I'm building my own island
in Second Life. // Girlfriend: Second
Life? **Get a life**!* • *Chico: Estoy
construyendo mi propia isla en
Second Life. // ¿Second Life? ¡Estás
colgao!*

get busy *loc.*

1 BAILAR, MOVER
EL ESQUELETO

—*DJ: Everybody **get busy** down
there!* • *DJ: ¡Todo el mundo a
mover el esqueleto ahí abajo!*

2 ECHAR UN POLVO

—*Come on, baby, let's **get busy**.* •
Vamos a echar un polvo, guapa.

get fitted _v._
MAQUEARSE, ARREGLARSE

—*I see you **got fitted**.* • *Veo que te has maqueado.*

get it _v._
1 ENTENDER, PILLAR, PISPAR

—*Do you **get it**?* • *¿Lo pillas?*

2 get it on _loc._
ECHAR UN POLVO

—*We were just about to **get it on** when my dad walked in.* • *Estábamos a punto de echar un polvo cuando entró mi padre.*

get off _v._
PONERSE CACHONDO/A, EXCITARSE

—*Hey, you pervert! Are you **getting off** on this?* • *¡Qué pervertido! Esto te pone, ¿no?*

get one's finger out _loc._
PONERSE LAS PILAS, ESPABILAR
La frase completa es **get one's finger out of one's arse**, o sea, literalmente "sacarse el dedo del culo".

—*The boss: Johnson, **get your finger out**.* • *El jefe: Johnson, espabila.*

get one's shit together _v._
RECOGER, PONER EN ORDEN, ORGANIZARSE

—*Come on! **Get your shit together**. We're out of here.* • *¡Venga! Recoge tus cosas, que nos vamos.*

get real _expr._
BAJA A LA TIERRA

—***Get real**, dude!* • *¡Tío, baja a la tierra!*

ghetto _n., adj._
1 GUETO, BARRIO

—*I was brought up in the **ghetto** and I'm proud of it* • *Crecí en un barrio pobre y estoy muy orgulloso de ello.*

2 CUTRE

—*That look is so **ghetto**!* • *¡Ese "look" es tan cutre!*

2 ghetto blaster _n._
LORO

—*Who's that asshole with the **ghetto blaster**? Yo! Turn it down now or I'll call the pigs!* • *¿Quién es ese gilipollas del loro? ¡Eh! ¡Baja el volumen o llamo a la pasma!*

ghi *acron.*
(gotta have it)
TENGO QUE TENERLO, ME LO VOY A PILLAR

—*sms 1: New CoD gold on mndy. // sms 2: GHI.* • *sms1: El nuevo "Call of Duty" sale el lunes. // sms 2: Me lo voy a pillar.*

gig *n.*
BOLO, CONCIERTO

—*When's your next gig?* • *¿Cuándo es vuestro próximo bolo?*

git [UK] *n.*
GILIPOLLAS

—*Move your arse, you git!* • *¡Mueve el culo, gilipollas!*

give lip *v.*
LLEVAR LA CONTRARIA

—*Don't give me lip boy or I'll deck you!* • *¡No me lleves la contraria o vas a cobrar!*

gladrags *n.*
LAS MEJORES GALAS

—*Get your gladrags on! We're going out on the town.* • *¡Ponte tus mejores galas! Nos vamos de fiesta a la ciudad.*

glued *adj.*
PEGADO/A, ENGANCHADO/A

—*You just sit their all day glued to the telly. Come on, get your finger out and get down the dole office.* • *Te pasas el día pegado a la tele. Vamos, mueve el culo y vete a la oficina del paro.*

go commando *loc.*
IR SIN GAYUMBOS
Expresión originalmente de uso militar que últimamente se ha puesto muy de moda entre diseñadores, periodistas, etc.

—*Nice kilt, Jock. Are you going commando?* • *Bonito "kilt", Jock. ¿Vas sin gayumbos?*

go juice *n.*
CAFÉ

—*Gimme some more go juice, man!* • *Dame más café , tío.*

go pear-shaped *loc.*
IRSE AL GARETE, IRSE A LA MIERDA

—*Then Martha walked in and it all went pear-shaped.* • *Luego entró Marta y todo se fue al garete.*

gob *n., v.*
1 BOCA, MORROS, PICO

—*Shut your gob!* • *¡Cierra el pico!*

2 ESCUPIR

—*Seeing somebody gobbing makes me puke.* • *Ver escupir a la peña me da mucho asco.*

gobshite *n.*

BOCAS, BOCAZAS

—*Shut it you* **gobshite**! *You talk nothing but crap.* • *¡Cállate bocazas! ¡No dices más que gilipolleces!*

go getter *n.*

ESPABILADO/A, ECHADO/A PA' LANTE

—*She's a real* **go getter**. • *Es muy espabilada.*

good and proper *loc.*

A SACO, DE LO LINDO

—*I'm gonna do him* **good and proper**. • *Le voy a dar de lo lindo.*

good to go *adj.*

LISTO/A, PREPARADO/A

—*Wife: You ready?* // *Husband:* **Good to go**, *babes.* • *Mujer: ¿Estás listo?* // *Marido: Listo, cariño.*

goodies (get the) *loc.*

MOJAR, FOLLAR

—*Did you* **get the goodies**? • *¿Mojaste?*

goof around *v.*

HACER EL TONTO

—*Stop* **goofing around**. *I want this by this afternoon.* • *Deja de hacer el tonto. Quiero esto para esta tarde.*

goof up *v.*

CAGARLA, PIFIARLA

—*Damn! I* **goofed up**. *I'm so sorry.* • *¡Mierda! La he cagado. Lo siento mucho.*

goof juice *n.*

PRIVA, BEBIDA

—*Waaashaaap?* // *Have you been on the* **goof juice**? • *¿Qué "pasha"?* // *¿Has estado privando?*

google *v.*

BUSCAR EN GOOGLE

—*Where's Kazakhstan?* // *Dunno.* **Google** *it.* • *¿Dónde está Kazajstán?* // *No sé. Búscalo en google.*

goose *v.*

PELLIZCAR EL CULO

—*Johnson's talking to that bird. Go up and* **goose** *him.* • *Johnson está hablando con esa tía. Acércate y pellízcale el culo.*

gotcha *interj.*

LO PILLO, TE SIGO

—*You got that?* // *Yeah, I* **gotcha**! • *¿Me sigues?* // *Sí, te sigo.*

gov' [UK] *n.*

JEFE

—*Ok,* **gov'**. *I'm nearly there.* • *Vale, jefe, ya casi estoy.*

granny panties *n.*
BRAGAZAS DE ABUELA

—*Oh, no!* **Granny panties.** *That's such a turn off!* • *¡Mierda! ¡Bragazas de abuela! ¡Qué bajón!*

grass *v., n.*
1 CHIVARSE, CANTAR

—*Did you* **grass** *on me?* • *¿Te has chivado de mí?*

2 HIERBA, MARÍA

—*I got some* **grass.** *You got any skins?* • *Tengo hierba. ¿Tienes un papel?*

gratz *abrev.*
(congratulations)
ENHORABUENA, FELICIDADES

—*Blue Baboon: gg // Green Goblin:* **Gratz!** • *Blue Baboon: Buena partida. // Green Goblin: ¡Enhorabuena!*

gravy train *n.*
UN CHOLLO DE TRABAJO

—*I'm back on the* **gravy train.** • *Vuelvo a mi chollo de trabajo.*

grease monkey *n.*
MECÁNICO

—*I'm taking my wheels to the* **grease monkey.** • *Llevo mi buga al mecánico.*

greasy spoon *n.*
Bar o cafetería un poco cutre y sucio pero con atractivo.

—*I'll have to warn you, it's a* **greasy spoon** *but you'll like it.* • *Tengo que avisarte, el sitio es un poco grasiento, pero te gustará.*

green *adj., n.*
1 VERDE, INEXPERTO/A

—*He's a bit* **green** *but he'll learn.* • *Está un poco verde, pero ya aprenderá.*

2 PASTA, GUITA

—*Show me the* **green.** • *Enséñame la pasta.*

3 HIERBA, MARÍA

—*Hey, I got some* **green** *for your bong.* • *Oye, tengo maría para tu arguila.*

grief *v.*
FASTIDIAR, JOROBAR
Este verbo está muy de moda en los mundos virtuales de internet.

—*I've been* **griefed** *again in Second Life.* • *Me han jorobado otra vez en Second Life.*

grind *n., v.*
1 LO NUESTRO, LO DE SIEMPRE

—*Right, guys! Break's over. Back to the* **grind.** • *¡Venga, chicos! Se acabó el descanso, volvamos a lo nuestro.*

2 ESFORZARSE, CURRÁRSELO

—*We **grind** all day and that fat cat gets all the lolly. Life's shit, then you die.* • *Nosotros nos lo curramos todo el día y el cerdo ese se lleva toda la pasta. ¡Qué injusta es la vida!*

groggy *adj.*
EMPANADO/A, GROGUI, SOPA

—*Sorry, I'm a bit **groggy** today.* • *Lo siento, estoy un poco empanao hoy.*

grounded *adj.*
CASTIGADO/A

—*I can't go out tonight. I'm **grounded**.* • *No puedo salir esta noche. Estoy castigado.*

gross [USA] *adj.*
ASQUEROSO/A

—*Girl: Don't do that! That's **gross**! // Boyfriend picking his nose: Okey-dokey.* • *Chica: ¡No hagas eso! ¡Es asqueroso! // Novio haciendo pelotillas en la nariz: Vale.*

grow a set *expr.*
ÉCHALE COJONES

—*Come on, Johnson. **Grow a set** and tell him to eff off.* • *Venga, Johnson. Échale cojones y mándale a la mierda.*

grub *n.*
COMIDA, PAPEO

—*The **grub**'s great in that pub. Wanna go?* • *Se come muy bien en ese pub. ¿Quieres ir?*

guff *v., n.*

1 TIRARSE UN PEDO

—*What's that smell? Who **guffed**?* • *¿Y ese olor? ¿Quién se ha tirado un pedo?*

2 PESTE A PEDO

—*What's that **guff**? Who cut one?* • *¡Qué peste! ¿Quién se ha bufado?*

3 CHORRADAS, TONTERÍAS

—*You're talking **guff**.* • *Vaya chorradas que dices.*

gun (son of a) *loc.*
HIJO DE TU MADRE

Para evitar decir **son of a bitch** se puede sustituir **bitch** por **gun**.

—*You **son of a gun**. I'ma gonna get you!* • *¡Hijo de... tu madre, te voy a dar!*

gung-ho *adj.*
ENTUSIASMADO/A, ESTAR POR LA LABOR DE HACER ALGO

—*Michael and Sarah aren't very **gung-ho** on helping me.* • *Michael y Sarah no están muy por la labor de ayudarme.*

¡Qué resaca! // John: No pasa nada,
tío, tú lo que necesitas es un remedio
alcohólico.

hairy *adj.*

ESPANTOSO/A, QUE PONE LOS
PELOS DE PUNTA, QUE ACOJONA

—That was a really **hairy** expe-
rience. • Eso fue una experiencia
espantosa.

half-assed [USA] *adj.*

CHAPUCERO/A, SIN ACABAR

—I'm phoning the workies tomorrow. They've left me with this **half-
assed** repair job. • Mañana llamo
a los paletas. Me han dejado colgado
con una chapuza a medias.

**EN INGLÉS BRITÁNICO
SE ESCRIBE
HALF-ARSED**

hacked-off *adj.*

MOSQUEADO/A, CABREADO/A

—Martha's **hacked off**. What
happened? • Marta está mosqueada.
¿Qué ha pasado?

hair band *n.*

Término que se usa para referirse
a las bandas heavies de los 80
cuyas prioridades eran las melenas
y los estridentes solos de guitarra
(en el mejor de los casos) o de
teclado (en el peor); grupos como
Mötley Crüe, Poison, Europe,
L.A. Guns, etc.

hair of the dog *n.*

Remedio para combatir la resaca
que consiste en volver a beber.

—Bill: Oh, no! I've got a hangover
// John: No problem, mate. What you
need is a **hair of the dog**! • Bill:

ham it up *v.*

SOBREACTUAR

—Actor: There's nothing wrong with
hamming it up a bit. • Actor: No
pasa nada con sobreactuar un poco.

handbags at dawn *loc.*

RIÑA, PELEA, DISCUSIÓN

Viene de la expresión **pistols at
dawn** ("duelos al amanecer"). La
sustitución de **pistols** ("pistolas")
por **handbags** ("bolsos") ridicu-

liza su significado por lo que da a entender que es una contienda poco seria, de poca monta.

—*A ding-dong? Nah, it was more like **handbags at dawn**.* • *¿Una bronca? No, fue más bien una discusión de poca monta.*

handle *n.*

1 NICK

—*My new **handle** is Blue Baboon.* • *Mi nuevo nick es Blue Baboon.*

2 love handles *n.*

MICHELINES SEXYS

—***Love handles** turn me on.* • *Los michelines me ponen.*

hang out *v.*

PASAR TIEMPO EN UN LUGAR, FRECUENTAR

—*We used to **hang out** at that pub for a while.* • *Por algún tiempo solíamos frecuentar aquel garito.*

hanky panky *n.*

FOLLETEO, ÑACA-ÑACA

—*I'm going out. No **hanky panky** when I'm gone, ok?* • *Voy a salir. Nada de ñaca-ñaca cuando esté fuera, ¿vale?*

hard on *n.*

EMPALMADA, SUBIDÓN

—*I've got a **hard on** for you the size of Peru.* • *Tengo un subidón del tamaño de Perú.*

hard-up *adj.*

PELADO/A, SIN BLANCA

—*I can't splash any cash. I'm **hard-up** at the moment.* • *No puedo soltar ni un duro. Ahora mismo estoy pelado.*

hash *n.*

1 COSTO, CHOCOLATE

—*Is that weed or **hash**?* • *¿Es hierba o costo?*

2 hash brownies *n.*

BROWNIES DE "CHOCOLATE"

—*I can make you some **hash brownies** if you don't smoke.* • *Te puedo hacer unos brownies de "chocolate" si no fumas.*

haul ass *expr.*

MUEVE EL CULO

—*Come on! **Haul ass**! We're outta here.* • *¡Venga! ¡Mueve el culo! Nos vamos.*

have kittens *expr.*

COMERSE EL TARRO

—*Why didn't you call? I was **having kittens**.* • *¿Por qué no has llamado? Ya me estaba comiendo el tarro.*

hawk *n.*

MANTERO/A, LATERO/A

—*You'll get it cheaper from the **hawks** in the centre.* • *Lo conseguirás más barato de los manteros del centro.*

heads are gonna roll _expr._

VAN A RODAR CABEZAS

—_That's the third contract we've lost._ **Heads are gonna roll.** • _Es el tercer contrato que perdemos. Van a rodar cabezas._

heart on _n._

Estado de euforia provocado por el efecto del amor, la pasión, o cualquier cosa que guste o emocione al corazón. Una especie de subidón de adrenalina.

—_Baby you give me such a_ **heart on.** • _Cari me pones el corazón a cien._

heaving _adj._

A PETAR, HASTA LA BANDERA, HASTA LOS TOPES

—_Come on. Let's go. It's_ **heaving** _in here._ • _Vámonos que esto está a petar._

heavy _adj._

1 DE PUTA MADRE

—_You passed? That's_ **heavy!** • _¿Aprobaste, no? ¡De puta madre!_

2 MUY SERIO, DURO, GRAVE

—_This is a_ **heavy** _situation. I don't know what to do._ • _Esto es muy grave. No sé que hacer._

heebie jeebies _n._

MIEDO, CAGUE, JIÑE

—_Let's get out of here! This place gives me the_ **heebie jeebies.** • _¡Vámonos! Este sitio me da cague._

hell yeah _interj._

PUES CLARO, DESDE LUEGO

—_Another beer?_ **Hell yeah!** • _¿Otra birra? ¡Pues claro!_

helluva _adv., adj._ (hell of a)

1 MUY, SUPER

—_Mike is a_ **helluva** _nice guy._ • _Mike es muy buen tío._

2 Como adjetivo puede utilizarse para destacar algo positivo o negativo.

—_That's a_ **helluva** _car he's got._ • _Pedazo de coche que tiene._

—_He has a_ **helluva** _life._ • _Tiene una vida muy dura._

hen party _n._

DESPEDIDA DE SOLTERA

—_It's like a fish market in here. Is that a_ **hen party?** • _Cuánta fémina suelta. ¿Hay una despedida de soltera?_

henpecked _adj._

CALZONAZOS

—_He's gonna call her indoors. He's_

henpecked. • *Es un calzonazos. Va a llamar a la parienta*

her indoors [UK] *n.*
LA MUJER, LA PARIENTA

—*I'm just gonna call **her indoors**.* • *Voy a llamar la parienta.*

hickey *n.*
CHUPETÓN

—*Hey! Is that a **hickey** you've got?* • *¡Oye! ¿Eso de ahí es un chupetón?*

high *adj.*

1 DROGADO/A, FUMADO/A, COLOCADO/A

—*Oh, man! I'm **high**.* • *¡Joder, tío! Vaya colocón.*

2 high and dry *adj.*
TIRADO/A, EN LA ESTACADA

—*Where were you? You left me **high and dry**!* • *¿Dónde estabas? ¡Me dejaste tirado!*

hip *adj.*
FASHION, LO MÁS

—*Flares are **hip** now.* • *Los pantalones de campana ahora son lo más.*

hissy fit *n.*
NUMERITO

—*Johnson's taking another **hissy fit**.* • *Johnson ya está montando otro numerito de los suyos.*

hit *n.*

1 ASESINATO

—*The head honcho ordered the **hit**.* • *El gran jefe dio la orden de asesinato.*

2 CALADA, TIRO

*Gimme a **hit**, man.* • *Dame una calada, tío.*

hit it *interj.*

1 DALE, VAMOS ALLÁ

—*Bruce Springsteen: Ok, Clarence, **hit it!*** • *Bruce Springsteen: Vamos, Clarence, ¡dale!*

2 SALIR CAGANDO LECHES, SALIR PITANDO

—*Bank robber: Come on! **Hit it!*** • *Ladrón de banco: ¡Vámonos de aquí cagando leches!*

hit on *v.*
TIRAR LOS TEJOS

—*Are you **hitting on** me?* • *¿Me estás tirando los tejos?*

hit the books *loc.*
HINCAR LOS CODOS

—*Come on! Let's **hit the books**.* • *¡Venga! ¡A hincar los codos!*

hit the door *loc.*
ABRIRSE, LARGARSE

—***Hit the door**, man!* • *¡Largémonos, tío!*

hit the road *loc.*
ABRIRSE, LARGARSE, SALIR
POR PATAS

—**Hit the road**, Jack. And, don't
you come back no more. • Lárgate,
Jack, y no vuelvas más.

hit the sack *loc.*
IRSE A LA PILTRA, IRSE AL
SOBRE

—I went straight home and **hit the
sack**. • Fui directamente a casa y
me metí al sobre.

hit the streets *loc.*
SALIR A LA LUZ, ESTAR EN
LA CALLE

—When this news **hits the streets**,
we're in deep shit! • Cuando esta
noticia salga a la luz, estaremos de
mierdo hasta el cuello.

hit the town *loc.*
SALIR DE FIESTA

—When we got to NYC, we **hit
the town** right away. • Nada más
llegar a Nueva York, nos fuimos de
fiesta.

ho *n. (vul.)*
PUTA, ZORRA

hockey mom *n.*
aka "soccer mom"
En los Estados Unidos estos
términos definen a una mujer de
clase media que vive en barrios
residenciales, que normalmente
no trabaja fuera de casa y su
única labor es llevar a los hijos
a sus partidos de hockey, fútbol,
baseball, etc., o a clases de música
o idiomas. Es la auténtica
Mrs. Average de este país.

hog *v.*
MONOPOLIZAR

—Hurry up! Stop **hogging** the
computer! • ¡Date prisa! ¡Deja de
monopolizar el ordenador!

hold up *v.*
1 ATRACAR, ASALTAR

—He got 5 years for **holding up** a
bank. • Le cayeron 5 años por atracar un banco.

2 RETRASAR, DETENER

—We were **held up** by heavy
traffic. • Nos hemos retrasado por
culpa del tráfico.

hold your horses *expr.*
PARA EL CARRO

—Just **hold your horses**! Let's
think about this. • ¡Para el carro!
Pensémoslo bien.

holla *v.*
LLAMAR, DAR UN TOQUE

—If you need anything, just **holla**. •
Si necesitas algo, dame un toque.

homeboy *n.*
AMIGUETE, COLEGA

—Hey, **homeboy!** Wassup! • ¡Qué pasa, colega!

honcho *n.*
LÍDER, JEFE

—Have some respect, brother! You're talking to the head **honcho** there. • ¡Ten un poco más de respeto, amigo! Estás hablando con el jefe!

hood *n.*
BARRIO

—I'm going up the **hood** to see my man. • Voy al barrio a ver a mi contacto.

hoodie *n.*
1 SUDADERA CON CAPUCHA

—He was wearing a white **hoodie**. • Llevaba una sudadera blanca con capucha.

2 Término usado para referirse a cierto tipo de delincuentes comunes, derivado del hecho de que muchos llevan sudaderas con capucha.

—Don't go down the mall, it's full of **hoodies**. • No vayas al centro comercial, está lleno de esos gamberros.

hoodlum *n.*
GAMBERRO, MACARRA

—Piss off, you **hoodlum!** • ¡Vete a la mierda, macarra!

hook *n.*
1 La parte más guay, que más se engancha, de una canción.

—Listen to this, the **hook's** coming up. • Escucha a eso, ya viene la parte guay.

2 GANCHO, PUÑETAZO

—I hit him with a good left **hook**. • Le di un buen gancho con el puño izquierdo.

3 hooked *adj.*
ENGANCHADO/A

—I'm totally **hooked** on season 3. • Estoy totalmente enganchado a la tercera temporada.

4 hook up with *loc.*
QUEDAR, VERSE

—Let's **hook up** the next time you're in town. • A ver si nos vemos la próxima vez que estés en la ciudad.

ECHAR UN POLVETE

—*I **hooked up with** Lisa last night.* • *Eché un polvete con Lisa anoche.*

horny [UK] *adj.*

1 ESTAR BUENO/A

—*She is a **horny** chick.* • *Está muy buena.*

2 CACHONDO/A

—*That dress makes me **horny**.* • *Ese vestido me pone cachondo.*

hot *adj.*

1 ESTAR BUENO/A

—*Baby, you are **hot**!* • *¡Qué buena estás!*

2 ROBADO/A, MANGADO/A

—*Be careful, these goods are **hot**. Do you know what I mean?* • *Ten cuidado, esta mercancía es robada.*

3 QUE MOLA, GUAY

—*This place is **hot**, man!* • *¡Este sitio mola, tío!*

hot-desking *n.*

SISTEMA EN OFICINAS QUE CONSISTE EN COMPARTIR SITIOS DE TRABAJO

—*No, you don't have a workspace for yourself. You have to share. We have a **hot-desking** policy in this company.* • *No, no tienes un sitio de trabajo exclusivo para ti. En esta empresa tenemos una política de compartir las mesas.*

hottie *n.*

TÍO/A BUENO/A

—*He's such a **hottie**.* • *Está muy bueno el tío.*

hump *v., n.*

1 MACHACAR

—*We got **humped** 6-0!* • *¡Nos machacaron 6 a 0!*

2 FOLLAR *(vul.)*

—*We **humped** all night.* • *Follamos toda la noche.*

3 CABREO

—*He's got the **hump**.* • *¡Vaya cabreo que lleva!*

humungous *adj.*

ENORME, SUPERGANSO/A

—*I had this **humungous** sandwich for lunch.* • *Me tomé un bocadillo superganso para comer.*

hung up *adj.*

MUY PILLADO/A POR ALGUIEN

—*Madonna: I'm **hung up**, I'm hung up on you.* • *Madonna: Estoy muy pillada, estoy muy pillada por ti.*

hunk *n.*

TÍO BUENO

—*Beckham's such a **hunk**!* • *¡Beckham está buenísimo!*

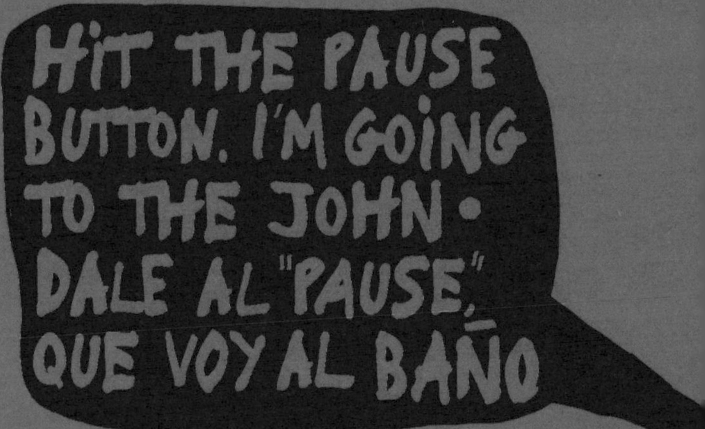
HIT THE PAUSE BUTTON. I'M GOING TO THE JOHN.
DALE AL "PAUSE", QUE VOY AL BAÑO

ice *n., v.*

1 DIAMANTES

—*Nice **ice**, dudette!* • *¡Bonitos diamantes, nena!*

2 SPEED, DROGA SINTÉTICA

—*I need a fix. Got any **ice**?* • *Necesito meterme algo, ¿tienes speed?*

3 CARGARSE, LIQUIDAR
Muy utilizado en series y pelis policiacas.

—*Detective: What happened to him?* // *Cop: He got **iced**.* • *Detective: ¿Qué le pasó?* // *Poli: Se lo cargaron.*

ice cold *n.*

BIRRA

—*Gimme an **ice cold**.* • *Ponme una birra.*

idiot box *n.*

TELE, CAJA TONTA

—*I'm gonna veg out in front of the **idiot box** tonite.* • *Esta noche voy a vegetar enfrente de la caja tonta.*

idk *acron.*
(I don't know)

NO LO SÉ

—*sms 1: CU 2nite?* // *sms 2: **idk**.* • *sms 1: ¿Nos vemos esta noche?* // *sms 2: No lo sé.*

iffy *adj.*

CHUNGO/A, SOSPECHOSO/A

—*Be careful! He looks a bit **iffy**.* • *¡Ten cuidado! No parece muy de fiar.*

ill *adj., v.*

1 GUAY, DE PUTA MADRE

—*That's **ill**, dude!* • *¡De puta madre, tío!*

2 RELAJARSE

—*Hey! I'm giving you a licence to **ill**, brother.* • *¡Oye! Te doy licencia para relajarte, hermano.*

I'm friends with that *expr.*

VALE, DE ACUERDO,
YA ME VA BIEN

—*Girlfriend: It's over!* // *Boyfriend: **I'm friends with that**.* • *Novia: ¡Hemos acabado!* // *Novio: Vale.*

I'm over it *expr.*
ME DA IGUAL, YA LO HE SUPERADO

—*Your ex has just walked in.* || **I'm over it**. • *Tu ex acaba de entrar.* || *Me da igual.*

I'ma [USA] *abrev.*
(I am going to)
VOY A

—**I'ma** *whip your ass!* • *¡Te voy a dar!*

imo *acron.*
(in my opinion)
EN MI OPINIÓN, PARA MÍ

—*sms 1: The new fcbk?* || *sms 2:* **imo** *gr8.* • *sms 1: ¿Qué tal el nuevo facebook?* || *sms 2: En mi opinión, buenísimo.*

in bed *expr.*
HACER NEGOCIOS JUNTOS, COLABORAR

—*Director: Now that Sony and Sanyo are* **in bed**, *we're up against it.* • *Director: Ahora que Sony y Sanyo hacen negocios juntos, lo tenemos crudo.*

innit? [UK]
(isn't it?)
¿VERDAD?, ¿NO?

—*It's cold in here,* **innit?** • *Hace frío aquí, ¿no?*

inside job *n.*
DELITO COMETIDO POR ALGUIEN DE DENTRO

—*All the evidence points to an* **inside job**. • *Todo apunta a que ha sido alguien de dentro.*

inside man *n.*
CONTACTO

—*Where did you get that info?* || *From my* **inside man**. • *¿De dónde has sacado esta información?* || *De mi contacto.*

inter-robbed *adj.*
ROBADO/A POR INTERNET

—*I got* **inter-robbed** *before I could cancel my cards.* • *Me robaron por internet antes de que pudiese cancelar mis tarjetas.*

itch for *v.*
MORIRSE DE GANAS

—*I'm* **itching for** *it to happen.* • *Me muero de ganas de que pase.*

itchy feet *adj.*
INQUIETO/A

—*I'm getting* **itchy feet**. *I need a new challenge.* • *Estoy inquieto. Necesito un reto nuevo.*

item *n.*
PAREJA

—*Are you two an* **item**? • *¿Sois pareja?*

*probably **jacking off** again.* • *Compañero de piso 1: ¿Qué está haciendo Jim allí?* // *Compañero de piso 2: Estará cascándosela otra vez.*

6 jack shit *n.*
NADA DE NADA, UNA MIERDA

—*Hey, meatball! You don't know **jack shit**!* • *¡Oye, muermo! ¡Tú no sabes una mierda!*

7 jackass *n.*
GILIPOLLAS

—*What are you doing, **jackass**?* • *¿Qué haces, gilipollas?*

jack *v., n.*

1 CHORIZAR, MANGAR
—*My jacket was **jacked** at the disco.* • *Me mangaron la chupa en la disco.*

2 PASTA
—*Got no **jack**, man!* • *No tengo pasta, tío.*

3 [USA] PITI, CIGARRO
—*Got a **jack**, bud?* • *¿Tienes un piti, colega?*

4 jack in *v.*
DEJAR, ABANDONAR, RENDIRSE

—*I've just **jacked** my job **in**.* • *Acabo de dejar el trabajo.*

5 jack off *v. (vul.)*
CASCÁRSELA

—*Housemate 1: What's Jim doing in there?* // *Housemate 2: Oh, he's*

jam *v.*

1 TOCAR MÚSICA IMPROVISANDO
—*They're **jamming** in the bar tonite. Wanna play?* • *Va a haber una "jam session" en el bar esta noche. ¿Quieres tocar?*

2 ESCUCHAR MÚSICA
—*Come over to mine tonite for some **jamming**.* • *Vente a casa a escuchar música.*

3 RELAJARSE CON AMIGOS
—*We're just **jamming** tonite at Pete's place. Wanna come?* • *Nos quedaremos de "relax" en casa de Pete esta noche. ¿Quieres venir?*

jammy *adj.*
QUE TIENE POTRA

—*You **jammy** git!* • *¡Qué potra tienes, cabrón!*

jet *v.*
SALIR PITANDO, ABRIRSE

—*Ok, guys! Let's jet.* • *¡Venga tíos, salgamos pitando!*

j/k *acron.*
(just kidding)
ES BROMA

—*sms 1: FU! || sms 2: j/k* • *sms 1: Que te den! || sms 2: Es broma.*

Jock [UK] *n.*
1 Término utilizado por los ingleses para referirse a los escoceses.

—*Hey, Jock! Where's your kilt?* • *¡Oye, Jock! ¿Dónde está tu falda?*

2 Jock rock *n.*
Término utilizado para referirse a la música rock escocesa en general.

—*Teenage Fanclub and two other Jock rock bands are in town.* • *Hoy tocan Teenage Fanclub y otros dos grupos escoceses.*

joe sixpack [USA] *n.*
Es el nombre que recibe un estereotipo estadounidense que se ha demostrado clave en las elecciones de los últimos años puesto que es el arquetipo de voto fluctuante. Hace referencia el americano medio: varón, blanco, trabajador, normalmente sin estudios universitarios y a menudo enamorado de la cerveza de lata (de ahí viene su nombre, del paquete de cervezas **sixpack**) y las retransmisiones deportivas.

john [USA] *n.*
VÁTER, BAÑO

—*Hit the pause button. I'm going to the john.* • *Dale al "pause", que voy al baño.*

johnny [UK] *n.*
CONDÓN, GOMA

—*No johnny, no action.* • *Sin condón, no hay acción.*

joint *n.*
1 PORRO, PETA

—*Pass the joint, dude. You're hogging it.* • *Que rule el porro, colega, lo estás monopolizando.*

2 LOCAL, LUGAR, GARITO

—*I really like this joint.* • *Me encanta este local.*

jugs *n. pl.*
TETAS, DOMINGAS

—*Look at those jugs! They're humungous!* • *¡Mira qué tetas! ¡Son enormes!*

HAY MUCHAS PALABRAS PARA DESIGNAR "TETAS": BOOBS, HOOTERS, JUBBLIES, MAMS, TITS...

DON'T KNOCK IT IF YOU HAVEN'T TRIED IT • NO LO CRITIQUES SI NO LO HAS PROBADO

kick off *v.*
EMPEZAR

—When does the party **kick off**? • ¿Cuándo empieza la fiesta?

kickin' *adj.*
DE PUTA MADRE, BRUTAL

—This party is **kickin'**, man. • Esta fiesta es de puta madre, tío.

kid *v.*
ESTAR DE CACHONDEO, BROMEAR

—I'm just **kidding**. • ¡Es broma!

killer, killa *adj.*
DE PUTA MADRE, BRUTAL

—That's a **killa** tune. • Este tema es brutal.

kinky *adj.*
PERVERTIDO/A, OBSCENO/A

—I heard he likes it **kinky**. • Me han dicho que le molan las cosas raras en la cama.

kip [UK] *v., n.*
1 DORMIR, SOBAR

2 SIESTA, CABEZADITA

—I'm gonna have a **kip**. • Voy a echar una cabezadita.

3 CAMA, PILTRA, SOBRE

—I'm going to my **kip**. • Me voy a la piltra.

kit *acron.*
(keep in touch)
ESTAMOS EN CONTACTO

—sms 1: c u l8a • sms 2: **kit** • sms 1: Hasta luego. || sms 2: Estamos en contacto.

kit *n.*
ROPA, TRAPOS

—Get your **kit** off! • ¡Quítate la ropa!

klutz *adj.*
TORPE, PATOSO/A

—You **klutz**! You've ballsed it up again. • ¡Qué torpe! ¡La has vuelto a cagar!

knackered _adj._
HECHO/A POLVO,
DESTROZADO/A

—I'm **knackered**. • Estoy hecha
polvo.

knob _n., v._
1 POLLA _(vul.)_

—**Knob** down the disco: Do you
wanna see my **knob**? // Girl: Piss
off! • El típico capullo de discoteca:
¿Quieres ver mi polla? // Chica: ¡Vete
a la mierda!

2 CAPULLO/A, GILIPOLLAS

—You **knob**! What did you do that
for? • ¡Oye, capullo! ¿A qué venía
eso?

3 TIRARSE A ALGUIEN _(vul.)_

—Are you **knobbing** that bird from
accounts? • ¿Te estás tirando a esa
tía de contabilidad?

knock _v._
1 CRITICAR

—Don't **knock** it if you haven't
tried it. • No lo critiques si no lo has
probado.

2 knock off [UK] _v._
FALSIFICAR

—I can **knock off** a few copies
before it hits the streets. • Puedo
falsificar unos cuantos ejemplares
antes de que vea la luz.

3 knock up _v._
PREÑAR, DEJAR EMBARAZADA

—I see her from next door is up the
duff again. Who **knocked** her **up**
this time? • Veo que la de al lado
está preñada otra vez. ¿Quién ha
sido esta vez?

knuckle down _v._
PONERSE A TRABAJAR,
PONERSE EN MARCHA,
PONERSE LAS PILAS

—Johnson, just **knuckle down** and
finish the job ASAP. • Johnson,
ponte las pilas y termina el trabajo
cuanto antes.

knucklehead _n._
CEPORRO/A, TONTOLABA

—You **knucklehead**! You always
balls it up. • ¡Tontolaba! Siempre
la cagas.

kthxbye _acron._
(ok thanks bye)
VALE ,GRACIAS, ADIÓS

—sms 1: C U soon // sms 2:
KTHXBYE • sms 1: Hasta pronto.
// sms 2:Vale, gracias, adiós.

kudos _n._
ENHORABUENA

—Level 20? **Kudos** 2u. • ¿Has superado el nivel 20? Enhorabuena.

label whore *n.*

ESCLAVO/A DE LAS MARCAS

—*Laura: Check my new adidas trainers.* // *Dakota: You're such a **label whore**!* • *Laura: Mira mis nuevas adidas.* // *Dakota: ¡Eres una esclava de las marcas!*

lad mag *n.*

REVISTA PARA HOMBRES

—*Friend: What's that?* // *Sue: Oh, it's just one of those **lad mags**.* • *Amigo: ¿Qué es eso?* // *Sue: Nada, una de esas revistas para tíos.*

lads [UK] *n.*

COLEGAS, LA PEÑA

—*Girlfriend: Where are you going?* // *Boyfriend: Oh, just out with the **lads**.* • *Novia: ¿Adónde vas?* // *Novio: Por ahí con los colegas.*

lame *adj.*

CUTRE, PATÉTICO/A, MALO/A, TONTO/A

—*That's a **lame** excuse.* • *¡Qué excusa tan mala!*

laters [UK] *expr.*

HASTA LUEGO

—*Jim: Right, guys. I'm off.* // *The guys: **Laters**!* • *Jim: Bueno, chicos. Me piro.* // *Los colegas: ¡Hasta luego!*

leak (take a) *loc.*

ECHAR UNA MEADA

—*I'm gonna **take a leak** first.* • *Voy a echar una meada primero.*

leet

El **leet** o **leet speak** es un tipo de escritura utilizada en internet que se caracteriza por mezclar letras, números y símbolos. Este tipo de escritura se puede configurar de varias formas, pero todas ellas emplean caracteres muy parecidos. Por ejemplo: 5 en lugar de S, 7 en lugar de T, 9 en lugar de G, etc. El **leet speak** está muy de moda entre los 933I<s (**geeks**) y los (-)4xx0rz (**hackers**).

lifer *n.*

ALGUIEN QUE TRABAJA EN LO MISMO TODA LA VIDA

—*Is old John still there?* // *Yeah, he's a **lifer**.* • *¿Sigue trabajando ahí el viejo John?* // *Sí, de allí ya no le mueve nadie.*

lift *v.*

1 PILLAR, DETENER

—*I got **lifted** for selling knocked off Guccis.* • *Me han pillado por vender Guccis falsos.*

2 ROBAR, CHORIZAR, MANGAR

—*Who **lifted** my mp3?* • *¿Quién me ha mangado el mp3?*

light up *v.*

FUMAR

—*You can't **light up** till you're outside the building.* • *No puedes fumar hasta que no estés fuera del edificio.*

like

Muletilla muy utilizada en la lengua oral, especialmente entre jóvenes estadounidenses.

—*I'm **like**, you can't do that, and he was **like**, are you sure?, so, I'm **like**, yeah!* • *Entonces yo le digo, eso no se puede hacer, y me dice, ¿seguro?, y yo, ¡pues claro!*

lip service (pay) *loc.*

DECIR UNA COSA Y HACER LO CONTRARIO

—*We will not tolerate governments who only **pay lip service** to this agreement.* • *No aceptaremos a esos gobiernos que hagan lo contrario de lo que prometen en este acuerdo.*

lmfao *acron.*
(laughing my fat arse off)

ME PARTO EL CULO GORDO DE RISA

lmtao *acron.*
(laughing my thin arse off)

ME PARTO EL CULO DELGADO DE RISA

lmaao *acron.*
(laughing my average arse off)

ME PARTO EL CULO NORMAL DE RISA

Estos acrónimos se usan sobre todo en SMS, en chats, etc. En este caso, la forma en la que uno se puede partir el culo de risa dependerá de la perspectiva del tamaño del culo.

loaf [UK] *n.*

CEREBRO, COCO, TARRO

—*Use your **loaf**, mate!* • *¡Usa el cerebro, colega!*

lol *acron.*
(laughing out loud)

JA JA JA

—*sms 1: U R dfcd! // sms 2: **LOL*** • *sms 1: Te he quitado de mi facebook. // sms 2: Jajaja.*

loony *n.*
PIRADO/A, CHALADO/A

—*You're a **loony**. You're not coming out with us again!* • *Tú estás pirao. ¡Nunca más vienes con nosotros!*

loopy *adj.*
PIRADO/A, COMO UNA CABRA

—*This guy's real **loopy**. He's freaking me out. Let's go!* • *Este tío está como una cabra. Me está acojonando. ¡Vámonos de aquí!*

lousy *adj.*
HORROROSO/A, CUTRE

—*And all I got was this **lousy** T-shirt.* • *Y todo lo que conseguí fue esta camiseta horrorosa.*

lovely jubbly *interj.*
GENIAL, PERFECTO

—*Julian: Here's an ice cold. // Lindsay: **Lovely jubbly!*** • *Julian: Toma una birra. // Lindsay: ¡Genial!*

lowdown *n.*
SECRETO, TOP SECRET

—*Keep this on the **lowdown**. Ok?* • *Esto es top secret, ¿eh?*

low-fi *adj.*
Término para referirse a música grabada utilizando poca tecnología

—*The first album was a **low-fi** classic. But now they've sold out.* • *El primer álbum fue un clásico del "low-fi", pero ahora se han vendido.*

low-key *adj.*
DISCRETO/A

—*Oh, it's just gonna be a **low-key** celebration. Just family and a few friends.* • *Va a ser una celebración discreta, solo la familia y algunos amigos.*

lylab *acron.*
(love you like a brother)
TE QUIERO COMO A UN HERMANO

—*sms 1: I miss U // sms 2: **lylab**.* • *sms 1: Te echo de menos. // sms 2: Te quiero como a un hermano.*

lylas *acron.*
(love you like a sister)
TE QUIERO COMO A UNA HERMANA

—*sms 1: I miss U // sms 2: **lylas**.* • *sms 1: Te echo de menos. // sms 2: Te quiero como a una hermana.*

main _adj._

FAVORITO/A, PREFERIDO/A

—You're my **main** man! • _¡Eres mi favorito!_

make my day _expr._

ADELANTE

—You want a fight? **Make my day!** • _¿Buscas pelea? ¡Adelante!_

make out _v._

ENROLLARSE (SEXUALMENTE)

—Let's **make out!** • _¡Enrollémonos!_

manky _adj._

MUY SUCIO/A, REPUGNANTE

—You've got a **manky** mind • _Tienes una mente muy sucia._

mardy _adj._

GRUÑÓN/A, CASCARRABIAS

—She's a **mardy** little cow. • _Es muy gruñona y además tiene mala leche._

mashed _adj._

CIEGO/A, PUESTO/A

—Leave him where he is. He's **mashed**. He'll get over it. • _Déjale, que va muy ciego. Ya se le pasará._

mate [UK] _n._

COLEGA, TRONCO, TÍO

—Alright, **mate**? • _¡Qué pasa, tronco!_

measly _adj._

MÍSERO/A, DE MIERDA

—I get this **measly** wage and that fat cat's rolling in it. • _Yo recibo este sueldo de mierda y a ese cerdo capitalista le sobra la pasta._

meatspace _n._

EL MUNDO REAL

En los mundos virtuales, el mundo verdadero o real se conoce como **meatspace** (literalmente "espacio de carne").

—I feel way more comfortable in Second Life than in **meatspace**. • _Me siento mucho más cómodo en Second Life que en el mundo real._

meaty *adj.*

DE BUENA CALIDAD, DE PUTA MADRE, COJONUDO/A

—*You'll like this next track. It's really **meaty**.* • *Te gustará el siguiente tema. Es cojonudo.*

mega *adj.*

SUPER, MEGA, HIPER

—*I'm saving up for a **mega** set of decks.* • *Estoy ahorrando para comprarme una supermesa de cambios.*

mental *adj.*

1 LOCO/A, PIRADO/A

—*You're **mental**!* • *¡Estás pirao!*

2 ENFADADO/A, CABREADO/A

—*Martha went **mental** when she found out.* • *Martha se cabreó cuando se enteró.*

3 BRUTAL

—*Great, innit? //**Mental**!* • *Genial, ¿no? //¡Brutal!*

mickey-mouse *adj.*

DE PACOTILLA

—***Mickey-mouse** referees are ruining this game.* • *Estos árbitros de pacotilla se están cargando este deporte.*

military precision *loc. adv.*

PRECISIÓN DE CIRUJANO, A LA PERFECCIÓN

—*He always goes about his business with **military precision**.* • *Siempre hace las cosas a la perfección.*

minger *n.*

CARDO, CALLO

—*This place is full of **mingers**. Let's go!* • *Este sitio está lleno de cardos. ¡Vámonos!*

minted *adj.*

FORRADO/A

—*The drinks are on me. I'm **minted** this week.* • *Las copas corren de mi cuenta, que esta semana estoy forrado.*

mmorpg *acron.* (massively-multiplaying online role-playing game)

JUEGO DE ROL EN LÍNEA JUGADO DE FORMA MÚLTIPLE Y MASIVA

—*Little brother: What's WoW? //Big brother: It's "World of Warcraft" and it's a **mmorpg**. Now, could you get out of my room, please?* • *Hermano pequeño: ¿Qué es WoW? //Hermano mayor: Significa "World of Warcraft" y es un "mmorpg". ¿Puedes pirarte ya de mi habitación, por favor?*

mockumentary *n.*
FALSO DOCUMENTAL

—*"This is Spinal Tap" is a **mockumentary** about the fictional heavy-metal band Spinal Tap.* • *"This is Spinal Tap" es un falso documental sobre la banda de heavy-metal ficticia Spinal Tap.*

mofo *acron.*
(**motherfucker**)
HIJO DE PUTA

—*Right, you **mofo**! Get out of here!* • *¡Hijo de puta, lárgate!*

mojo *n.*
Originalmente **mojo** significaba "hechizo" o "conjuro", pero actualmente se traduciría, en función del contexto, como "talento", "inspiración", "autoestima" o "confianza". En algunos casos se podría traducir como "duende".

—*Has he lost his **mojo**?.* • *¿Ha perdido su "duende"?*

monkey (brass) [UK] *adj.*
UN FRÍO QUE PELA

—*It's **brass monkey** weather outside. I'm staying in.* • *Fuera hace un frío que pela. Yo paso de salir.*

moon *v.*
HACER UN CALVO

—*Sparky **mooned** them from the passenger window.* • *Sparky les hizo un calvo por la ventana del pasajero.*

motor *n.*
CARRO, BUGA

—*Hey, I can give you a lift in my **motor**.* • *Vamos que te llevo en mi buga.*

mouth off *v.*
1 IRSE DE LA LENGUA, LARGAR

—*Well, if you keep **mouthing off** all the time, nobody will tell you anything.* • *Como sigas largándolo todo, nadie te contará nada.*

1 FARDAR

—*He keeps **mouthing off** about his new car, his new iPhone, his new anything.* • *No para de fardar de su coche nuevo, de su iPhone nuevo, de todo lo nuevo que tiene.*

muck in *v.*
REPARTIR EL TRABAJO, APECHUGAR, ECHAR UNA MANO

—*Right, everybody **muck in** and we'll finish this today.* • *Venga, si todo el mundo apechuga acabaremos esto hoy.*

muck out *v.*
LIMPIAR LA CUADRA, LIMPIAR LA POCILGA

—*I know it's a bummer but we've got to **muck out** the flat before we* *leave.* • *Ya sé que es un palo pero tenemos que limpiar esta pocilga antes de irnos.*

muck up *v.*

CAGARLA, JODERLA

—*I've **mucked** it **up** again. Damn it!* • *La he cagado otra vez. ¡Mierda!.*

mug *n.*

TONTO/A, PARDILLO/A

—*You **mug**! She's been two-timing you for ages.* • *¡Qué tonto eres! Lleva poniéndote los cuernos desde hace tiempo.*

mull over *v.*

PENSAR ALGO BIEN, REFLEXIONAR

—*Ok, no hurry. **Mull** it **over** and give me your answer on Monday.* • *No hay prisa. Piénsalo bien y me das una respuesta el lunes.*

mullet *n.*

Esta palabra se refiere a esos peinados tan populares hace unos años que se caracterizaban por unas greñitas detrás y el pelo más o menos corto por delante y por los lados. Un bigotillo nunca desentona con un buen **mullet**. También se conoce como **business in the front, party in the back**.

—*Nice **mullet**!* • *¡Bonito peinado!*

munchies *n.*

EL HAMBRE QUE ENTRA DESPUÉS DE HABER FUMADO UN PORRO

—*I've got the **munchies**. What have you got in the fridge?* • *Vaya gusa que me ha entrado después del porrito. ¿Tienes algo en la nevera?*

muppet *n.*

CAPULLO, MELÓN

—*You **muppet**!* • *¡Capullo!*

muscle in *v.*

ENTROMETERSE, METERSE POR MEDIO CON PREPOTENCIA

—*I was doing OK till he **muscled in** and took her away.* • *Iba todo bien hasta que se metió por medio y se la llevó.*

mush *n.*

MORROS

—*Do you want a smack in the **mush**?* • *¿Quieres que te dé un hostión en los morros?*

n00b, noob, newbie *n.*

NOVATO/A (USADO SOBRE TODO ENTRE INTERNAUTAS)

—*You've been owned, **n00b**!* • *¡Te he machacado, novato!*

naff *adj.*

1 CUTRE, CURSI, HORTERA

—*This game's really **naff**.* • *Este juego es muy cutre.*

2 naff off *interj.*

VETE A LA MIERDA, ANDA YA

—*Knob down the disco: Hello! || Girl: **Naff off!*** • *El gilipollas de la disco: ¡Hello! || Chica: ¡Vete a la mierda!*

nancy boy *n.*

MARICA, MARIPOSA

—*Hey, **nancy boy**!* • *¡Eh, marica!*

narked *adj.*

MOSQUEADO/A, PICADO/A

—*What are you so **narked** about?* • *¿Por qué estás tan mosqueado?*

neat [USA] *adj.*

GENIAL, FANTÁSTICO/A, GUAY

—*It would be **neat** to learn about you.* • *Sería genial tener noticias tuyas.*

nerd *n.*

UN/A FRIQUI, UN/A COLGADO/A, UN BICHO RARO

—*Green Goblin: I've conquered Africa in World Conquest! || Girlfriend: You're a **nerd**. And, your name's not Green Goblin, it's John. And you're not a warrior, you're my boyfriend.* • *Duende verde: ¡He conquistado África en La Conquista del Mundo! || Novia: Eres un friqui; y no te llamas "Duende verde", te llamas John; además no eres un guerrero, eres mi novio.*

netiquette *n.*

NETIQUETA

Este término se refiere a las normas básicas de comportamiento que deben seguir los internautas en sus contactos virtuales.

netizen *n.*

CIUDADANO/A DE LA RED

networking *n.*
HACER CONTACTOS

—*What's Johnson doing talking to that minger?* || *He's **networking**... I guess.* • *¿Qué hace Johnson hablando con ese cardo?* || *Está haciendo contactos... supongo.*

nick *v., n.*

1 MANGAR, CHORIZAR

—*Who **nicked** my mp3?* • *¿Quién me ha mangado el mp3?*

2 TRINCAR A ALGUIEN POR CHORIZO

—*You're **nicked**!* • *¡Te hemos trincado!*

3 CHIRONA, COMISARÍA

—*Right, sunshine. Let's take you down the **nick**.* • *¡Vamos, gracioso! Te llevamos a chirona.*

4 ESTADO, CONDICIÓN

—*It's only had two careful lady owners and it's in good **nick** for its age.* • *Solo ha tenido dos propietarias muy cuidadosas y está en muy buen estado para los años que tiene.*

nickle-and-dime *adj.*
BARATO/A, TIRADO/A DE PRECIO

—*You'll get them cheaper down the **nickle-and-dime** store.* • *Los encontrarás más baratos en "los chinos".*

nifty *adj.*
COJONUDO/A, MUY GUAY

—*That's a **nifty** laptop.* • *Este portátil es cojonudo.*

nip *n.*
PEZÓN

—*Did you see Janet's **nips** on TV last night?* • *¿Viste los pezones de Janet en la tele anoche?*

no brainer *n.*
OBVIEDAD, PAN COMIDO

—*Deciding to sign for a club of this size and stature was a **no brainer**.* • *No hacía falta ser muy listo para decidir fichar por un club tan grande y con tanto nivel.*

no can do *expr.*
DE ESO NADA, NI LO SUEÑES

—*Can you phone the school and pretend you're my mum?* || ***No can do**.* • *¿Puedes llamar al cole y hacerte pasar por mi madre?* || *Ni lo sueñes.*

no show *n.*
AUSENTARSE, NO APARECER

—*The guest was a **no show**.* • *El invitado no apareció.*

no way *expr.*
NI DE COÑA, DE ESO NADA

—*There's **no way** I'm gonna do it.* • *Ni de coña voy a hacer eso.*

nookie *n.*

1 SEXO, UN POLVO

—*No **nookie** till you say sorry.* • *Nada de sexo hasta que no pidas perdón.*

2 nookie badge *n.*

CHUPETÓN

—*Is that a **nookie badge** on your neck?* • *¿Tienes un chupetón en el cuello?*

nosh [UK] *n.*

PAPEO, MANDUCA

—*I'm going to the greasy spoon for some **nosh**. Wanna come?* • *Voy al bar a papear algo. ¿Te vienes?*

not in my book *expr.*

POR AHÍ NO PASO

—*You don't do that! **Not in my book**!* • *¡No hagas eso! ¡Por ahi no paso!*

nowt *n.*

NADA

—*I don't owe nobody **nowt**.* • *No debo nada a nadie.*

En inglés coloquial es muy normal utilizar dos y hasta tres partículas negativas en una frase aunque la gramática lo prohíba.

nsa *acron.*
(no strings attached)

SIN ATADURAS, SIN COMPROMISO

—*sms: fncy a jb?* **NSA**. • *sms: ¿Quieres un trabajo? Sin compromiso.*

number one *n.*

UNO/A MISMO/A, MENDA

—*The first piece of advice is always look after **number one**.* • *El primer consejo es siempre cuidar de uno mismo.*

numpty *n.*

MAMONAZO, CAPULLO

—*Get out of here, you **numpty**!* • *¡Lárgate de aquí, mamonazo!*

nut *n., v.*

1 COCO

—*Use your **nut**, Johnson.* • *Usa el coco, Johnson.*

2 DAR UN CABEZAZO

—*Zidane has just **nutted** the Italian.* • *Zidane le acaba de dar un cabezazo al italiano.*

nutter *n.*

CHALADO/A, PIRADO/A

—*Your boyfriend's a **nutter**. You know that, don't you?* • *Tu novio es un chalado. Lo sabes, ¿no?*

od *n., v.*
(overdose)
1 SOBREDOSIS

2 PEGARSE UN ATRACÓN

—*We **OD**'d on movies last night.*
• *Nos pegamos un atracón de pelis anoche.*

odds-on *adj.*
SEGURO, FIJO

—***Odds-on** I win.* • *Fijo que gano.*

off the hook *adj.*
1 LIBRADO/A

—*Right, Johnson. You're **off the hook**. Some other muppet has owned up to it.* • *Vale, Johnson te has librado. Otro gilipollas ha admitido el delito.*

2 [USA] DE PUTA MADRE

—*The party was **off the hook**.* • *La fiesta estuvo de puta madre.*

okey-dokey *expr.*
VALE, DESDE LUEGO

Versión más jocosa e informal de la archiconocida y supermega usada en todo el mundo mundial **OK**.

—*Boss: I want it on my desk by this afternoon. || Johnson: **Okey-dokey**.*
• *Jefe: Lo quiero encima de mi mesa antes de esta tarde. || Johnson: Vale.*

old-school *adj.*
DE LA VIEJA ESCUELA, ANTICUADO/A

—*I can tape it for you. || Tape it? Don't you mean burn it? You're so **old school**.* • *Te lo puedo grabar en una cinta. || ¿Una cinta? ¿Querrás decir un CD? Estás tan anticuado.*

omg *acron.*
(oh my god!)
¡DIOS MÍO!

—*sms 1: $1000 4U. || sms 2: **OMG**!*
• *sms 1: 1000 $ para ti. || sms 2: ¡Dios mío!*

on ice *loc. adv.*
EN STAND-BY, PARADO/A

—*Journalist: What about some European gigs? || Jay Z: Well, touring's **on ice** at the mo'.* • *Periodista: ¿Y conciertos europeos? || Jay Z: Bueno, la gira está parada de momento.*

on the blink *loc. adv.*
ESTROPEADO/A

—*The telly's **on the blink** again.*
• *La tele está estropeada otra vez.*

on the cheap *loc. adv.*

DE FORMA BARATA, EN PLAN CUTRE

—*Daniel:Where can I get the dough to do all that? // Lee: I know a geezer who can get it done on the cheap.* • *Daniel: ¿Dónde consigo la pasta para hacer eso? // Lee: Conozco a un tío que te lo podría hacer barato.*

on the fly *loc. adv.*

DE EXTRANJIS, DE TAPADILLO

—*He's working on the fly and still drawing dole money.* • *Trabaja de extranjis y sigue cobrando el paro.*

on the house *loc. adv.*

A CUENTA DE LA CASA

—*The drinks are on the house.* • *Las copas corren a cuenta de la casa.*

one-cheek bench sneak *n.*

Pedo tirado muy discretamente levantando ligeramente uno de los cachetes del culo mientras se está sentado/a.

oomph *n.*

GANAS, ENERGÍA, ESFUERZO EXTRA

—*Come on, Johnson! Give it a bit of oomph!* • *¡Venga, Johnson! ¡Échale un poco de ganas!*

out *v., adj.*

1 Dar una información personal y confidencial en contra de la voluntad de la persona, provocando con ello su vergüenza o la pérdida de dignidad, estatus, amigos o dinero.

—*They were outed as terrorist collaborators on that web page.* • *En aquella web, sin prueba alguna se dijo de ellos que habían colaborado con terroristas.*

2 LO QUE NO ES "IN" ES "OUT"

—*No, darling! Not that one. That colour is out this summer.* • *¡No, cariño! Ese no. No se lleva ese color este verano.*

out of order *expr.*

INACEPTABLE, TE HAS PASADO

—*You called her what? You're out of order, mate. Step outside.* • *¿Que le llamaste qué? Te has pasado, colega.*

owned *adj.*

MACHACADO/A

—*You've been owned, n00bie!* • *¡Te he machacado, novato!*

own up to *v.*

ADMITIR, RECONOCER

—*Johnson, you're off the hook 'cos I owned up to it.You owe me a pint.* • *Johnson, te has librado porque lo he admitido yo. Me debes una pinta.*

THAT JOKE ISN'T FUNNY ANYMORE. IT'S SO PLAYED OUT!
•ESE CHISTE ESTÁ MUY SOBAO. YA NO TIENE GRACIA

patsy *n.*

1 PELELE

—*I'm no **patsy**. Go take the piss out of somebody else!* • *No soy un pelele. ¡Ve a tomarle el pelo a otro!*

2 CABEZA DE TURCO

—*Judge: Did you do it? // The accused: No, I was just the **patsy**, your honor. // Judge: I beg your pardon?* • *Juez: ¿Lo hizo? // Acusado: No, solo era el cabeza de turco, señoría. // Juez: ¿Cómo dice?*

3 COLGADO/A DE AMOR

—*I am just a **patsy** for your love.* • *Estoy colgado de tu amor.*

phat *adj.*

GUAY, LO MÁS, LA HOSTIA

—*Check this **phat** website.* • *Mira esta pasada de página web.*

phishing *n.*

Timo de internet que consiste en invitar a los internautas, bajo pretexto de facilitarles claves para acceder a su cuenta bancaria por internet, a visitar páginas web falsas haciéndoles creer que se encuentran en la original.

phoney *adj.*

FALSO/A, MENTIROSO/A

—*Don't listen to a word he says, he's so **phoney**.* • *No creas ni una palabra de lo que dice, es muy falso.*

piece *n.*

ARMA, PIPA

—*That's it! I'm gonna whack him. Get me my **piece**.* • *¡Ya está! Me lo voy a cargar. Pásame la pipa.*

pig *n.*
aka "the pigs"

PASMA, POLI, PICOLETO, PITUFO

—*Edge it! The **pigs** are here!* • *¡Al loro! ¡Ha llegado la pasma!*

HAY MUCHAS PALABRAS PARA REFERIRSE A LA POLI: BACON, FILTH, THE FUZZ ...

pig out *v.*

COMER COMO UN/A CERDO/A, PONERSE MORADO/A

—*We **pigged** out on pizza last night.* • *Nos pusimos morados de pizza anoche.*

pigsty *n.*

POCILGA

—Get this **pigsty** cleaned up now! •
¡Limpia esta pocilga ahora mismo!

pimp the system *loc.*

CHUPAR DEL ESTADO, VIVIR
DEL CUENTO

—He's unbelievable. Ten years
pimping the system. • Flipo con
este tío. Lleva 10 años viviendo del
cuento.

piss *v., n.*

1 MEAR

—The pigs caught me **pissing** in
the street. • Me pilló la poli meando
en la calle.

2 MEADA

—Hit the pause button. I'm going
for a **piss**. • Dale al "pause", que
voy a echar una meada.

piss about/around *v.*

1 VACILAR

—Are you **pissing** me **around**? •
¿Me estás vacilando?

2 RASCARSE LA BARRIGA

—The boss: Johnson! Stop **pissing
around**! I said, "by this afternoon",
remember? • El jefe: ¡Johnson! ¡Deja
de rascarte la barriga! Te he dicho
que lo necesitaba para esta tarde, ¿te
acuerdas?

piss down *v.*

CAER LA DE DIOS

—It's been **pissing down** since
Monday. • Desde el lunes que está
cayendo la de Dios.

piss head *n.*

BORRACHUZO/A

—He's always down the pub. He's a
piss head. • Siempre está en el bar,
es un borrachuzo.

piss off *interj.*

VETE A LA MIERDA

—You mofo! **Piss off**! • ¡Hijo de
puta! ¡Vete a la mierda!

pissed *adj.*

1 [USA] CABREADO/A, DE MALA
LECHE

—I'm so **pissed** at you, man! • ¡Estoy tan cabreado contigo, tío!

2 [UK] CIEGO/A, PEDO

—He can't speak. He's **pissed**. •
No puede hablar. Está ciego.

3 pissed off [UK] *adj.*

CABREADO/A, DE MALA HOSTIA

—I'm so **pissed off** at you! • ¡Estoy
muy cabreado contigo!

pisser n.
1 PUTADA

—*Working on a Saturday? What a **pisser**!* • *¿Trabajar un sábado? ¡Qué putada!*

2 MEADERO

—*Hit the pause button. I'm going to the **pisser**.* • *Dale al "pause", que voy al meadero.*

piss take n.
VACILADA, TOMADURA DE PELO

—*I can't believe this. It's a **piss take**.* • *Esto no me lo creo. Es una tomadura de pelo.*

piss up n.
CIEGO, CEBOLLÓN

—*Oh, look! Two full kegs! Let's have a **piss up**!* • *¡Mira! ¡Dos barriles llenos! ¡Pillemos un cebollón!*

pit n.
1 PILTRA, CATRE, SOBRE

—*I'm off to my **pit**.* • *Me voy a la piltra.*

2 ANTRO, CUCHITRIL

—*This place is a **pit**.* • *Este lugar es un cuchitril.*

plastered adj.
CIEGO/A, COCIDO/A, PEDO

—*Oh, man! I can't remember a thing. I was **plastered** last night.* • *¡Tío! No me acuerdo de nada. Iba muy pedo anoche.*

plastic n.
TARJETA, PLÁSTICO

—*I ain't got no dough on me. You take **plastic**?* • *No llevo pasta. ¿Aceptáis tarjeta?*

play away v.
TENER UNA AVENTURA, LIARSE

—*Yeah, she left him. He was **playing away**.* • *Sí, le dejó. Tenía una aventura con otra.*

play hooky v.
FUMARSE LA CLASE, HACER PELLAS, HACER CAMPANA

—*No wonder you failed. You **played hooky** all year.* • *No me extraña que hayas suspendido. Te has estado fumando las clases todo el año.*

played out adj.
SOBADO/A, REQUETEVISTO/A

—*That joke isn't funny anymore. It's so **played out**.* • *Ese chiste está muy sobao. Ya no hace gracia.*

plumbing n.
LAS CAÑERÍAS
También se utiliza para referirse al aparato reproductivo.

—*I need to get my **plumbing** seen to soon.* • *Necesito que me revisen las cañerías pronto. (Vamos, que necesita follar.)*

pokey *n., adj.*

1 CHIRONA, TALEGO

—*He spent twenty years in the **pokey** for whacking Big Bill Malone.* • *Pasó 20 años en chirona por cargarse a Big Bill Malone.*

2 PEQUEÑO/A E INCÓMODO/A, CUTRE, RAQUÍTICO/A

—*Got a room yet? // Yeah, it's a bit **pokey**, but it'll do till the summer.* • *¿Ya tienes habitación? // Sí, es un poco cutre, pero me bastará hasta el verano.*

ponce [UK] *n.*

MARICA

—*Hey, you **ponce**! Sit down!* • *¡Oye, marica! ¡Siéntate!*

pong *n.*

PESTAZO

—*What's that **pong**? Did you chuff?* • *¿Qué es ese pestazo? ¿Te has tirado un pedo?*

poof *n.(vul.)*

MARICA, BUJARRÓN

—*Gay man 1: Hey, you **poof**! // Gay man 2: Hi darling. Give me a kiss!* • *Gay 1: ¡Eh, maricón! // Gay 2: Hola, cariño. ¡Dame un beso!*

porkchop *n.*

HELICÓPTERO DE LA POLICÍA

—*Get inside! There's a **porkchop** up there.* • *¡Entrad! Hay un helicóptero de la pasma por ahí.*

pos *acron.*
(piece of shit)

CABRÓN/A, MIERDA

—*Game message 1: Eat it! // Game message 2: **POS*** • *¡Toma ya! // Cabrón.*

poser *n.*

UN POSTURITAS, FALSO/A

—*He ain't a rapper. He's a **poser**!* • *No es un rapero. Va de eso pero no lo es.*

pot *n.*

1 MARÍA, HIERBA

—*I've got my bong but no **pot**.* • *Tengo la arguila pero no tengo maría.*

2 pothead *n.*

FUMETA

—*Get your finger out, you **pothead** loser!* • *¡Mueve el culo, fumeta de mierda!*

preggers *adj.*

PREÑADA

—*I see her from next door is **preggers** again.* • *Veo que la vecina de enfrente está preñada otra vez.*

pre-nup *n.*

CONTRATO PRE-MATRIMONIAL

—Sign a **pre-nup** first. She's a gold digger. • Firma un contrato pre-matrimonial. Tiene pinta de que esta tía va por la pasta.

prick *n.*

MAMÓN/A, GILIPOLLAS

—Piss off, you **prick**! • ¡Vete a la mierda, mamón!

psycho *n.*

CHALADO/A

—You're a **psycho**. Let me out of here! • Eres un chalado. Déjame salir de aquí.

pube *n.*

PELOS PÚBICOS

—Irate flatmate: Listen, guys! Clean the shower after you! The sight of **pubes** makes me puke. • Compañera de piso furiosa: ¡Atención, tíos! ¡Limpiad la ducha después de usarla! Los pelos púbicos me dan mucho asco.

puke *v.*

POTAR

—Flatmate 1: Are you OK in there? // Flatmate 2: No, I just **puked**. • Compañero de piso 1: ¿Todo bien ahí dentro? // Compañero de piso 2: No, acabo de potar.

pull *v.*

LIGAR, PILLAR CACHO

—Did you **pull** last night? • ¿Ligaste anoche?

pumped *adj.*

LISTO/A, A TOPE

—Coach: Ready? // Captain: I'm **pumped**, boss! • Entrenador: ¿Estás preparado? // Capitán: ¡A tope, jefe!

punk [USA] *n.*

GILIPOLLAS, NIÑATO

—Listen, you **punk**. I want the scrilla before Friday. • Escucha, gilipollas, quiero la pasta antes del lunes.

pusher *n.*

CAMELLO

—Neighbour 1: Her from next door's a **pusher**. // Neighbour 2: No way! Neighbour 1: Way! • Vecino 1: La vecina de enfrente es camello.//Vecino 2: ¿En serio? //Vecino 1: ¡En serio!

pussy *n. (vul.)*

CHOCHO, POTORRO

—Knob down the disco: Hey, Lucy. Show me your **pussy**! // Girl: Naff off, you twat! • El gilipollas de la disco: Eh, Lucy. ¡Enséñame el chocho! // Chica: ¡Vete a la mierda!

mates at school. She's got her little entourage following her about wherever she goes. Can you believe it? • Mi hermana se ha convertido en la reina del insti. Tiene a un séquito de niñas que la siguen por todos lados. ¡Pa' flipar!

queer adj.
MARICA

—Get me a piña colada. By the way I'm not **queer**. • Ponme una piña colada. Por cierto, no soy marica.

quicky n.
POLVETE, QUIQUI

—Husband: Time for a **quicky**? I'm so randy. // Wife: No. • Marido: ¿Tenemos tiempo para un quiqui rápido? Estoy muy cachondo. // Mujer: No.

quack n.
MATASANOS

—Why do you go to that hospital? It's full of **quacks**! //Well, it's next to my house. • ¿Por qué vas a ese hospital? Está lleno de matasanos. // Es que está al lado de mi casa.

quarter-life crisis n.
Crisis de temprana edad (entre los 20 y los 30 años aproximadamente) provocada por la toma de grandes decisiones.

—James is suffering from a **quarter-life** crisis, but he doesn't know. • James padece una crisis de temprana de edad, pero aún no lo sabe.

queen bee n.
LA REINA, LA MÁS POPULAR

—My sis is the **queen bee** with her

quits n. pl.
EN PAZ

—Dave: That's us **quits**! // Ken: You're bamboozling me, mate. • Dave: Ya estamos en paz. // Ken: Me estás tomando el pelo, tío.

quote-unquote loc. adv.
SUPUESTAMENTE, ENTRE COMILLAS

—It was a fix, **quote-unquote**. • Supuestamente fue un montaje.

ralph v.

POTAR

—*Last night I **ralphed** for ten minutes straight.* • *Ayer por la noche poté sin parar durante 10 minutos.*

randy adj.

CACHONDO/A

—*Wife: Time for a quicky? I'm **randy**! // Husband: No, I have a headache.* • *Mujer: ¿Te hace un polvete? ¡Estoy cachonda! // Marido: No, tengo jaqueca.*

rat n.

1 SOPLÓN, CHIVATO/A

—*Give me the name of the **rat**.* • *Dame el nombre del soplón.*

2 CABRÓN, JETA

—*Daily News: Love **Rat** Leaves Wife For 20-year-old Bimbo.* •

Daily News: Cabrón deja a su esposa por una barbie de 20 años.

rat-arsed adj.

CIEGO/A

—*Oh, look! A crate of beer. Let's get **rat-arsed**!* • *¡Mira que mogollón de cerveza! ¡Pillemos un buen ciego!*

ratty adj.

DE MALA LECHE, CABREADO/A

—*What's making you so **ratty** today?* • *¿Por qué estás de tan mala leche hoy?*

red-eye flight n.

Vuelo que sale a altas de horas de la madrugada o muy pronto por la mañana. Recibe este nombre porque los pasajeros suelen llegar con los ojos enrojecidos por la falta de sueño.

—*I'm knackered. I've just had a **red-eye flight**.* • *Estoy destrozada. Me he pasado la noche en el avión.*

reefer n.

PORRO, PETA, CANUTO

—*Stop hogging the **reefer**, man. //* *Vale ya de monopolizar el porro, tío.*

retrosexual n.

Un hombre que gasta lo menos posible en su apariencia y cuidados físicos; algo así como lo contrario a un metrosexual.

—Girl: *Splash more cash on your look! I'm not asking you to be George Clooney, but just look decent!* // Boy: *I told you, I'm a* **retrosexual!** • Chica: *¡Cúrrate un poco tu aspecto! No te pido que seas George Clooney, pero al menos ve un poco decente!* // Chico:*Ya te lo dije, ¡soy "retrosexual"!*

right on *interj.*
DE PUTA MADRE

—Host: *Beers?* // *The lads:* **Right on!** • Anfitrión: *¿Unas birras?* // Los colegas: *¡De puta madre!*

ringtone dj *n.*
El típico pesado que siempre está rayando con los tonos del móvil.

—Teacher: *Right, who's the* **ringtone dj** *at the back?* • Profe:*Ya vale, ¿quién es el gracioso que le está dando a los "tonitos" del móvil allí atrás?*

rip *v.*
RIPEAR
Pasar pistas de música de formato CD a mp3.

—Pass me that CD. *I'm gonna* **rip** *it.* • Pásame el CD que lo voy a "ripear".

rip off *v., n.*
1 CLAVAR, TIMAR, TOMAR EL PELO

—You've been **ripped off**, *mate!* • ¡Te han timado, tío!

2 CLAVADA, TIMO, ESTAFA

—That's a **rip off!** • ¡Vaya timo!

rock *v.*
1 MOLAR, FLIPAR

—That **rocks!** • ¡Eso mola!

2 PASARLO PIPA

—We **rocked** *at the gig last night.* • Anoche lo pasamos pipa en el concierto.

rock on *interj.*
MUY BIEN, DE PUTA MADRE

—sms 1: *ding! LVL 16* // sms 2: **RCK on!** • sms 1: ¡Nivel 16! // sms 2: ¡Muy bien!

rock out *v.*

VOLVERSE LOCO/A BAILANDO, TOCANDO O ESCUCHANDO MÚSICA

—*What a gig! They really **rocked out**.* • *¡Qué pasada de concierto! ¡Cómo la liaron!*

rofl *acron.*
(rolling on the floor laughing)

JA JA JA

roll up, skin up *v.*

LIAR UN PORRO

—*Got any skins? I wanna **roll up**.* • *¿Tienes papel? Quiero liar un porro.*

rollin' *adj.*

COLOCADO/A, PUESTO/A, PASADO/A

—*Leave him lying there. He's **rollin'**.* • *Déjalo ahí tumbado, que va muy pasado.*

root for *v.*

ANIMAR, APOYAR, IR CON

—*I'll be **rooting for** Liverpool in the final.* • *Voy a ir con el Liverpool en la final.*

rpg *acron.*
(role-playing game)

JUEGO DE ROL

—*"Dungeons and Dragons" is one of the oldest **RPGs**.* • *"Dragones y Mazmorras" es uno de los juegos de rol más antiguos.*

rubber [USA] *n.*

1 CONDÓN, GOMA, CALCETÍN

—*No **rubber**, no action.* • *Sin condón, no hay acción.*

2 rubber bus *n.*

LÍNEA NOCTURNA DE AUTOBÚS URBANO

—*Will we get a taxi home? // No, the **rubber bus** will be along in a minute.* • *¿Vamos en taxi a casa? // No, el bus nocturno está a punto de llegar.*

3 rubber check *n.*

CHEQUE SIN FONDO

—*If you've no dough, I'm not accepting any of your **rubber checks**.* • *Si no tienes pasta, no acepto ninguno de tus cheques sin fondo.*

run-of-the-mill *adj.*

DEL MONTÓN, NORMAL

—*I'm just a **run-of-the-mill** kind of guy.* • *Solo soy un chico normal.*

rust bucket *n.*

TARTANA, CAFETERA (COCHE)

—*If you think I'm gonna get in that **rust bucket**, you are very much mistaken.* • *Si piensas que me voy a meter en esa tartana, estás muy equivocado.*

sack *n.*
CAMA, CATRE, PILTRA, SOBRE

—*I'm gonna hit the* **sack**. • *Me voy al sobre.*

sad *adj.*
COLGADO/A, PRINGADO/A

—*Blue Baboon: I've conquered Europe in "World Conquest"! // Girlfriend: You're* **sad**. • *Blue Baboon: He conquistado Europa en el "World Conquest". // Novia: ¡Tú estás colgado!*

saddo *n.*
PRINGADO/A

—*Blue Baboon: I'm going to invade Africa in "World Conquest" now! // Girlfriend:* **Saddo!** • *Blue baboon: ¡Ahora voy a invadir África en el "World Conquest"! // Novia: ¡Pringao!*

sap *n.*
PARDILLO/A

—*You* **sap**! • *¡Qué pardillo eres!*

sauce *n.*
1 ALCOHOL, PRIVA

—*Been on the* **sauce** *again? Come on, you piss head. I'll get you a taxi.* • *¿Otra vez dándole al alpiste? Venga, bolinga, que te pillo un taxi.*

2 **sauced** *adj.*
CIEGO/A, PEDO

—*Barman: I think it's time you went home. You're* **sauced**. • *Camarero: Creo que ya es hora de que te vayas a casa. Vas muy ciego.*

saucy *adj.*
SEXY, CAÑÓN

—*Have you seen that* **saucy** *bird in accounts?* • *¿Has visto a la tía cañón de contabilidad?*

sausage fest *n.*
A **sausage fest** es cuando en un lugar se juntan muchos hombres a la vez. El origen de la expresión no es difícil de adivinar.

—*Oh, no! Stag party alert! This is gonna be a* **sausage fest**. • *¡Mucho ojo! ¡Despedida de soltero! ¡Esto va a ser un campo de nabos!*

scene *n.*
ROLLO, ESCENA

—*I'm not really into this indie* **scene**. • *No me acaba de gustar este rollo "indie."*

school of hard knocks *n.*

LA ESCUELA DE LA VIDA

—*They don't tell you that at your uni. I learnt that from the **school of hard knocks**.* • *Eso no te lo enseñan en la universidad. Eso lo he aprendido en la escuela de la vida.*

scoff *v.*

DEVORAR, ENGULLIR, ZAMPARSE

—*Hey! You've **scoffed** the lot.* • *¡Eh! Te lo has zampado todo.*

score *v.*

1 PILLAR (DROGAS)

—*I'm going up the hood. I need to **score**.* • *Voy al barrio que necesito pillar.*

2 PILLAR CACHO, LIGAR

—*Did you **score** last night?* • *¿Pillaste cacho anoche?*

scrap *v., n.*

1 PELEARSE, ZURRARSE

—*Right, you two! Stop **scrapping** and get to bed.* • *¡Basta ya de zurraros vosotros dos e id a la cama ya!*

2 BRONCA, MOVIDA, PIRULA

—*There was a right **scrap** down the kebab shop last night.* • *Menuda bronca que se montó en la tienda de kebabs anoche.*

screw *v.*

1 JODER A ALGUIEN

—*Are you trying to **screw** me?* • *¿Intentas joderme?*

2 FOLLAR *(vul.)*

—*Wanna **screw**?* • *¿Quieres follar?*

3 screw up *v.*

JODERLA, CAGARLA

—*Sorry, I **screwed up**.* • *Lo siento, la he jodido.*

scrummy *adj.*

DELICIOSO/A, COJONUDO/A

—*Mary: Fancy some cake? || Mark: **Scrummy**!* • *Mary: ¿Te hace un poco de pastel? || Mark: ¡Cojonudo!*

scumbag *n.*

CABRÓN/A, DESGRACIADO/A

—*You **scumbag**!* • *¡Desgraciado!*

seal the deal *loc.*

CERRAR EL TRATO

—*Pass by the bar tonite and we'll **seal the deal**.* • *Pásate por el bar esta noche y cerramos el trato.*

search engine *n.*

BUSCADOR DE INTERNET

—*Do you know any good **search engines**?* • *¿Conoces algún buen buscador de internet?*

sell out *v.*

VENDERSE

—*Journalist: The new album goes against what you've done in the past and has a blatantly commercial sound. Won't the fans think you are **selling out**?* • *Periodista: El nuevo álbum es muy distinto de lo que habíais hecho hasta ahora y tiene un sonido de lo más comercial. ¿No van a pensar los fans que os habéis vendido?*

sexcellent *adj.*

ORGÁSMICO/A, SUBLIME

—*This chocolate cake is **sexcellent**!* • *¡Este pastel de chocolate es orgásmico!*

shack up *v.*

ARREJUNTARSE, IRSE A VIVIR CON ALGUIEN

—*I heard Kenny's **shacked up** with that bird.* • *Me han dicho que Kenny se ha ido a vivir con esa tía.*

shades *n. pl.*

GAFAS DE SOL

—*Like the **shades**, man! Are they Ray-Bans?* • *¡Me molan tus gafas de sol, tío! ¿Son Ray-Ban?*

shady *adj.*

1 CHUNGO/ A, SOSPECHOSO/A

—*She's a **shady** lady.* • *Es una mujer chunga.*

2 RESERVADO/A, CORTADO/A

—*Don't be so **shady**. Come in.* • *No seas tan cortado. Entra.*

shaft *v., n.*

1 JODER VIVO A ALGUIEN

—*This company's **shafting** us!* • *¡Esta empresa nos está jodiendo vivos!*

2 CEPILLARSE A ALGUIEN *(vul.)*

—*Are you **shafting** that bird from the pub?* • *¿Te estás cepillando a aquella tía del pub?*

3 POLLÓN *(vul.)*

—*Twat down the disco: Look at my big **shaft**! || Girl: Naff off!* • *El gilipollas de la disco: ¡Mira qué pollón tengo! || Chica: ¡Vete a la mierda!*

shag *v. (vul.)*

1 FOLLAR

—*Wanna **shag**?* • *¿Quieres follar?*

2 **shagged out** *adj.*

HECHO/A POLVO, DESTROZADO/A

—*Going down the pub, mate? || Nah, I'm **shagged out**!* • *¿Vienes al pub, tío? || No, estoy hecho polvo.*

shark *n.*

1 ESTAFADOR/A

—*Don't buy it from them. They're **sharks**.* • *No se lo compres a ellos. Son unos estafadores.*

2 UN CRACK, UN AS

—*Be careful before you put your money on the table. He's a pool **shark**.* • *Ten cuidado antes de poner el dinero en la mesa. Es un crack del billar.*

shattered *adj.*
HECHO/A POLVO, MUERTO/A

—*I'm staying in. I'm **shattered**.* • *Me quedo en casa. Estoy muerta.*

shebang (the whole) *n.*
TODO EL TINGLADO, ABSOLU-TAMENTE TODO

—*Detective Sergeant: How much do you wanna know, sir?* // *Detective Inspector: **The whole shebang**, my son.* • *Sargento: ¿Cuánto quiere saber, señor?* // *Inspector: Absolutamente todo, hijo.*

sheeple *n.*
BORREGO/A, SIN IDEAS PROPIAS

—*The problem with this country is that it's full of **sheeple**.* • *El problema de este país es que está lleno de borregos.*

shit *n.*
1 MIERDA

—***Shit**! I lost again.* • *¡Mierda! He vuelto a perder.*

2 COSAS, PERTENENCIAS

—*Have you seen my **shit**?* • *¿Has visto mis cosas?*

3 full of shit *loc.*
CHORRADAS, TONTERÍAS

—*Johnson, you're **full of shit**.* • *Johnson, no sabes ni lo que dices.*

4 when the shit hits the fan *expr.*
CUANDO SALGA TODA LA MIERDA A LA LUZ

—***When the shit hits the fan**, I'll take the blame.* • *Cuando salga toda la mierda a la luz, asumiré que es culpa mía.*

5 shit-hot *adj.*
COJONUDO/A, DE PUTA MADRE

—*Have you tried "World Conquest" on facebook? It's **shit-hot**!* • *¿Has probado ya el "World Conquest" de facebook? ¡Es cojonudo!*

6 shit happens *expr.*
COSAS QUE PASAN

—*I got a punch in the face for ordering a piña colada in that boozer.* // ***Shit happens**.* • *Me dieron un puñetazo por pedir una piña colada en ese bareto.* // *Cosas que pasan.*

shop *v.*
CHIVARSE

—*Who **shopped** me?* • *¿Quién se ha chivado?*

shove it up your arse *expr. (vul.)*
MÉTETELO DONDE TE QUEPA

—*Johnson: **Shove** your job **up your***

arse! • *Johnson: ¡Métete tu trabajo donde te quepa!*

silent but violent *adj.*
UN PEDO QUE NO SE OYE PERO SE HUELE

—*Oh, no! Who was that?* **Silent but violent.** *Open a window!* • *¡Joder! ¿Quién ha sido? "Silencioso pero violento". ¡Abre alguna ventana!*

sista *n.*
MUJER NEGRA, HERMANA

—*Yo,* **sista!** • *¡Hola, hermana!*

sixpack *n.*
TABLETA DE CHOCOLATE
Llamado así por el parecido a un pack de seis cervezas.

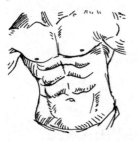

sketchy *adj.*
POCO CLARO/A, CON POCOS DETALLES

—*Detective sergeant: Right, I want the whole story.* // *Suspect: It's all a bit* **sketchy,** *I'm afraid.* • *Sargento: Bien, quiero toda la historia.* // *Sospechoso: Me temo que no está muy clara.*

skin *n.*

1 PAPEL DE FUMAR

—*Got any* **skins,** *mate?* • *¿Tienes papel, tío?*

2 CABEZA RAPADA, SKIN

—*He got beaten up by a bunch of* **skins.** • *Una panda de skins le dieron una paliza.*

skinny-dipping (go) *loc.*
BAÑARSE EN BOLAS

—*It was great! We all went* **skinny-dipping** *at midnight.* • *¡Fue genial! Nos bañamos en bolas a media noche.*

skint *adj.*
PELADO/A, SIN UN DURO

—*Going out tonight?* // *I can't. I'm* **skint.** • *¿Sales esta noche?* // *No puedo, no tengo ni un duro.*

slag off *v.*
PONER A PARIR

—*Husband: Darling, you're always* **slagging off** *other women.* // *Wife: No, I'm not.* • *Marido: Cariño, siempre estás poniendo a parir a otras mujeres.* // *Mujer: No es verdad.*

slam *v.*

1 PONER VERDE, DESPOTRICAR

—*The book was **slammed**.* • *Despotricaron del libro.*

2 FOLLAR, CEPILLARSE A ALGUIEN *(vul.)*

—*See her? I **slammed** her last week.* // *You're so full of shit!* • *¿Ves esa tía? Pues me la follé la semana pasada.* // *¡Qué gilipolleces dices!*

slammer *n.*

CHIRONA, TALEGO

—*Don't do it! You'll get 20 years in the **slammer** for whacking him.* • *¡No lo hagas! Te caerán 20 años en el talego si te lo cargas.*

slapper *n.*

ZORRA, PUTÓN, PUTILLA

—*Wife: Serena's just a **slapper**!* // *Husband: You're such a bitch.* • *Mujer: ¡Serena es una putilla!* // *Marido: Qué mala eres.*

MUCHAS SON LAS PALABRAS USADAS PARA DENOMINAR (METAFÓRICAMENTE O NO) LA PROFESIÓN MÁS ANTIGUA DEL MUNDO: SKANK, SLAG, SLUT, WORKING GIRL, HOOKER...

slash *n.*

MEADA

—*I'm going for a **slash**.* • *Voy a echar una meada.*

sleazy *adj.*

PERVERTIDO/A, OBSCENO/A

—*Get away from me you **sleazy** git!* • *¡Lárgate de aquí, pervertido de mierda!*

slick *adj.*

SUPERCOOL, SUPERGUAY

—*That is a **slick** set of decks!* • *¡Cómo molan estos platos!*

slog *n.*

CURRAZO, MACHACADA

—*This is a hard **slog**.* • *Esto es un currazo.*

smack *n.*

HEROÍNA, CABALLO

—*He's back on the **smack** again.* • *Ha vuelto al caballo.*

smarmy git *n.*

CREÍDO/A, PIJO/A, FANTASMA

—*He's showing off his car keys again.* // ***Smarmy git**!* • *Ya está fardando con las llaves de su coche otra vez.* // *¡Fantasma!*

smirt *v.*

(smoke + flirt)

Hace referencia al hecho de salir fuera de un pub donde no se puede fumar para fumarse un piti y aprovechar para ligar con otros/as fumadores/as.

—*I'm going to smirt.* • *Voy a fumar y a ver si hay suerte y pillo cacho.*

smitten *adj.*

ALUCINADO/A, FLIPADO/A

—*After a few dates Mark was totally smitten with Almu.* • *Tras un par de citas, Mark estaba totalmente flipado con Almu.*

sms *acron.*

(short message service)

La comunicación a través de sms ha creado un tipo de escritura especial en el cual letras y números reemplazan a palabras.

b = be
8 = ate
c = see
4 = for
r = are
2 = to / too
u = you
y = why
n = and

Combinando estos elementos podemos crear frases como las siguientes.

ur l8 = you are late
cu l8r = see you later
ru in = are you in?
y r u l8 = why are you late?
b4 9 = before nine
gr8 m8! = great mate!

Otra característica es que algunas letras, especialmente vocales, así como la puntuación desaparecen para economizar el mensaje.

facebook = fcbk
message = msg
please = plz
thanks = thx
text = txt
bck = back
thx 4 ur msg = thanks for your message

Otra característica es que por ejemplo -orr- y -ause- se transforman en -oz.

sorry = soz
because = coz

Abundan también los acrónimos.

idk = i don´t know
ttyl = talk to you later
btw = by the way

snafu *acron.*
(situation normal, all fucked-up)
SITUACIÓN JODIDA

snog *v.*
MORREARSE, PEGARSE EL LOTE

—*I saw you **snogging** that bloke from up the road.* • *Te he visto morrearte con ese tío del barrio.*

snot *n.*
MOCOS

—*Blow your nose! You've got **snot** running down.* • *Suénate la nariz que tienes mocos.*

snuff *v.*
MORIR, PALMARLA

—*Is he still alive?* || *Nah, he **snuffed** it years ago.* • *¿Aún está vivo?* || *No, la palmó hace años.*

so over *loc.*
SUPERACABADO/A

—*I'm **so over** you. Go away!* • *Lo nuestro está más que acabado. ¡Lárgate!*

so yesterday *loc.*
PASADO DE MODA, DEL AÑO DE LA PERA

—*That joke is **so yesterday**.* • *Ese chiste es del año la pera.*

sob *acron.*
(son of a bitch)
HIJO DE PUTA

—*gamer 1: You've been owned!* || *gamer 2: **SOB**.* • *Jugador 1: Te he ganado.* || *Jugador 2: Hijo de puta.*

solid *adj.*
DE PUTA MADRE, EXCELENTE

—*Boss: Can I trust him?* || *Worker: Yeah, he's **solid**.* • *Jefe: ¿Me puedo fiar de él?* || *Trabajador: Sí, es un tío de puta madre.*

space cadet *n.*
EMPANADO/A, QUE ESTÁ EN LA LUNA

—*He's a **space cadet**!* • *¡Es un empanao!*

spaced out *adj.*
1 DISTRAÍDO/A, COLGADO/A, EN LAS NUBES

—*What's wrong with you today? You're **spaced out**.* • *¿Qué te pasa hoy? Estás empanao.*

2 COLOCADO/A

—*Take him home. He's **spaced out**, man.* • *Llévalo a casa. Está colocado.*

spike *v.*
PONER ALCOHOL O DROGA A UNA BEBIDA

—*James Bond: You've **spiked** my drink.* || *Bond girl: Goodnight,*

James. • *James Bond: Has puesto droga en mi bebida.* // *Chica Bond: Buenas noches, James.*

spin *v.*

1 MENTIR, INVENTARSE HISTORIAS

—*Are you **spinning** again?* • *¿Estás mintiendo otra vez?*

2 PINCHAR

—*And, **spinning** on the wheels of steel... DJ Flash!* • *Y, pinchando esta noche... ¡DJ Flash!*

3 EXAGERAR O DISTORSIONAR UNA NOTICIA

Este es un uso muy habitual entre periodistas, expertos en marketing, etc.

4 UNA VUELTA EN COCHE

—*Fancy a **spin** in my new motor?* • *¿Te hace una vuelta en mi buga nuevo?*

splash the cash *expr.*

SOLTAR LA PASTA

—*I've just **splashed the cash** for my girlfriend's birthday.* • *Acabo de soltar pasta para el cumple de mi novia.*

spliff *n.*

1 PORRO, PETA

—*Fancy a **spliff**?* • *¿Te hace un porrito?*

2 spliff up *v.*

FUMAR UN PORRO

—*Here's a skin. **Spliff up**.* • *Toma, un papel. Fumemos un canuto.*

spot on *adj.*

PERFECTO/A, EXACTO/A

—*Is that OK?* // *Spot on!* • *¿Está bien?* // *¡Perfecto!*

square *n.*

1 MUERMO, COÑAZO, TOSTÓN

—*You're such a **square**!* • *¡Eres tan muermo!*

2 [USA] PITI

—*Bum me a **square**, man.* • *Dame un piti, tío.*

squeeze *n.*

AMIGO/A CON DERECHO A ROCE

—*Are you two an item?* // *No, he's just my latest **squeeze**.* • *¿Sois pareja?* // *No, es solo un amigo con derecho a roce.*

stag party *n.*

DESPEDIDA DE SOLTERO

—*Sausage alert! Here comes the **stag party**.* • *¡Cuidado! Aquí viene la despedida del soltero.*

steaming *adj.*

PEDO, CIEGO/A

—*Barman: I can't serve you any*

*more drink, mate. You're **steaming**.
Go home.* • *Camarero: No te puedo
servir más, amigo. Estás pedo. Vete
a casa.*

step (it) up *v.*

ESPABILARSE

—*Come on, guys! **Step it up**. Two
hours till the deadline.* • *¡Venga, chicos! Espabilad que solo nos quedan
dos horas para entregarlo.*

stingy *adj.*

AGARRADO/A, TACAÑO/A, RATA

—*Splash the cash, you **stingy** git!* •
¡Suelta la pasta, agarrado!

stitch up *loc. v.*

TOMAR EL PELO

—*He gave me 10, I gave him 2,
then he gave his 2 to her.* // *Lovely
jubbly. You really **stitched** him **up**
this time.* • *Me dio 10, yo le di 2 y
luego él le dio 2 a ella.* // *Genial. Le
has tomado el pelo de verdad esta
vez.*

stoned *adj.*

FUMADO/A

—*Step out of the car, sir. You look a
bit **stoned**.* • *Salga del coche, señor,
parece que va un poco fumado.*

stoner *n.*

PORRETA, FUMETA

—*Get a life, you **stoner**!* • *¡Búscate
la vida, porreta!*

stonking *adv.*

PEDAZO DE, MUY

—*And there was this **stonking**
great big hole in the road.* • *Y
había un pedazo de socavón en la
carretera.*

straight *adj.*

1 HETERO

—*Are you **straight** or are you gay?*
• *¿Eres hetero o gay?*

2 LIMPIO/A

—*Doctor: How long have you been
straight? // Ex junkie: About 3
months now.* • *Doctor: ¿Cuánto
tiempo llevas limpio? // Ex yonqui:
Unos 3 meses.*

3 get things straight *expr.*

DEJAR LAS COSAS CLARAS

—*Let's talk and **get things
straight**.* • *Hablemos y dejemos
las cosas claras.*

street cred *n.*

REPUTACIÓN, IMAGEN

—*Kid, you can't hang out with me.
I have my **street cred** to think
about.* • *Chaval, no puedes ir por
ahí conmigo. No es bueno para mi
reputación.*

stuff *n.*

COSAS, PERTENENCIAS,
ASUNTOS

—*Where's my **stuff**?* • *¿Dónde están
mis cosas?*

suck _v._

1 SER UNA MIERDA, UN ROLLO

—This music **sucks**. • Esta música es una mierda.

2 suck ass _loc._

SER UNA MIERDA PINCHADA EN UN PALO

—This music **sucks ass!** • ¡Esta música es una mierda pinchada en un palo!

3 suck face _loc._

MORREARSE, DARSE EL LOTE

—How would you know? You two were **sucking face** all night long. • ¿Cómo lo vais a saber si estuvisteis toda la noche morreándoos?

4 suck up to _loc._

HACER LA PELOTA

—**Sucking up to** teacher again? • ¿Ya estás otra vez haciéndole la pelota al profe?

sucker _n._

PRINGADO/A, MEMO/A

—Wise up, **sucker!** • ¡Ponte serio, pringao!

s'up? _abrev._ (What's up?)

¿QUÉ PASA?

suss out _v._

1 PILLAR, ENTERARSE

—She finally **sussed out** what was going on. • Al final pilló lo que estaba pasando.

2 sussed (out) _adj._

CALADO/A, CONTROLADO/A

—I've got her **sussed**. • La tengo calada.

—Don't you worry about a thing. I've got it all **sussed**. • No te preocupes por nada. Lo tengo todo controlado.

swag _n._

ROPA, ESTILO, LOOK

—Dig the **swag!** • ¡Me mola tu look!

swanky _adj._

SUPERGUAY

—That's a **swanky** bike, man. • ¡Es superguay esta moto, tío!

swift one _n._

UNA COPA O BIRRA RÁPIDA

—Time for a **swift one?** • ¿Tienes tiempo para una copa rápida?

swing _v._

HACER INTERCAMBIOS DE PAREJAS

—I heard they **swing** at their parties. • Me han dicho que hacen intercambios de parejas en sus fiestas.

IF YOU WANT IT, YOU CAN WHISTLE FOR IT• SI LO QUIERES, YA PUEDES ESPERAR SENTADO

tab *n.*

1 PASTI

—Got any **tabs**? • ¿Tienes pastis?

2 [UK] PITI

—Got a **tab**, mate? • ¿Tienes un piti?

tackle *n.*

PAQUETE, PELOTAS

—Footballer: Watch my **tackle**! • Futbolista: ¡Cuidado con mis pelotas!

tacky *adj.*

CUTRE

—Her house is so **tacky**! • ¡Su casa es tan cutre!

talk shit *loc.*

DECIR TONTERÍAS, DECIR CHORRADAS

—You are **talking shit**, man! • ¡No digas tonterías, tío!

talk to the hand *expr.*

PASO DE TI

—Sparky: Are you listening to me? // Mhairi: **Talk to the hand**! • Sparky: ¿Me estás escuchando? // Mhairi: ¡Paso de ti!

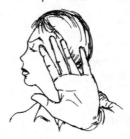

telly *n.*

TELE

—I'm just gonna veg out in front of the **telly**. • Voy a vegetar un poco delante de la tele.

text *v.*

MANDAR UN SMS

—**Text** me! • ¡Mándame un sms!

thang *n.*

COSA

—Give me, give me my **thang**. Baby, just give me some more. ("My Thang", James Brown) • Dame, dame mi "cosa". Cariño, dame más.

throwback *n.*

1 UN FRIQUI DE LO RETRO

—*How can I describe him? Well, he's a 70s* **throwback.** • *¿Cómo podría describirlo? Bueno, es un friqui de los setenta.*

2 REVIVAL, ALGO QUE TE HACE RECORDAR UNA ÉPOCA DEL PASADO

—*That's a* **throwback** *to my school days.* • *Eso es como volver a la época del cole.*

thumb *v.*

MANDAR UN SMS

—**Thumb** *me!* • *¡Mándame un sms!*

thumb through *v.*

HOJEAR

—*I saw this great article when I was* **thumbing through** *paper.* • *Vi un artículo superbueno mientras hojeaba el periódico.*

tick off *v.*

1 CHINCHAR, FASTIDIAR

—*Why are you* **ticking** *me* **off** *all the time?* • *¿Por qué me estás chinchando todo el rato?*

2 MONTAR UN POLLO

—*She gave him a right* **ticking off** *last night.* • *Ayer por la noche le montó un pollo tremendo.*

tide over *v.*

IR TIRANDO, APAÑÁRSELAS

—*I'm skint. Can you give me a few dollars to* **tide** *me* **over** *till pay day?* • *Estoy pelado. ¿Me prestas unos dólares para ir tirando hasta que cobre?*

tight *adj.*

ÍNTIMO/A

—*Hey, brother! We're* **tight,** *ain't we?* • *¡Oye, hermano! Somos íntimos, ¿no?*

tip off *v.*

IRSE DE LA LENGUA

—*Do you know who* **tipped** *us* **off?** • *¿Sabes quién se ha ido de la lengua sobre lo nuestro?*

toast *adj.*

JODIDO/A

—*We're* **toast!** • *¡Estamos jodidos!*

toke *n.*

UN TIRO, UN TIRITO, UNA CALADA

—*Want a* **toke** *on this, dude?* • *¿Quieres un tiro de esto, tío?*

tool *n.*

GILIPOLLAS, CAPULLO/A

—*You* **tool!** • *¡Qué gilipollas eres!*

totty _n._

TÍA BUENA, PIBÓN

—Loads of **totty** here tonight. •
Mucha tía buena por aquí hoy.

toy boy _n._

YOGURÍN, BOLLICAO

—That's her from next door with
her **toyboy**. • Esa es la vecina de
enfrente con su yogurín.

tranny _n._

TRAVELO

—The **trannies** are fighting again!
I don't know whether to call the
police or Almodóvar. • Las travelos
están peleándose otra vez. No sé si
llamar a la poli o a Almodóvar.

trippy _adj._

RARÍSIMO/A, ALUCINANTE,
SURREALISTA

—I'm sure I've been here before!
No? This is **trippy**! • Estoy seguro
que ya había estado aquí antes! ¿No?
¡Qué raro todo!

ts _acron._
(tough shit)

TE JODES, HAY QUE JODERSE

—sms1: I got owned in WoW //
sms 2: **TS**! • sms 1: Me ganaron en
el WoW. // sms 2: ¡Te jodes!

tuck (it) away _v._

NO PARAR DE COMER

—I've been **tucking** it **away**
lately, man. • Tío, últimamente no
paro de comer.

tuppence worth [UK] _n._

METER BAZA, DECIR LA SUYA

—He always has to get his **tuppen-
ce worth** in. • Siempre tiene que
decir la suya.

turf _n._

TERRITORIO

—They whacked him on his own
turf. • Se lo cargaron en su propio
territorio.

twat _n._

GILIPOLLAS, MAMÓN/A,
CAPULLO/A

—Hey! You **twat**! • ¡Oye! ¡Mamonazo!

two-time _v._

PONER LOS CUERNOS, PONER
LOS TOCHOS

—Did you know that creep was
two-timing me? He'll get what's
coming. • ¿Sabías que ese capullo me
estaba poniendo los cuernos? Ahora
se va a enterar.

uber *adv.*
SUPER

—*That place is **uber** cool.* • *Ese sitio es supercool.*

uglify *v.*
AFEAR

—*You have to leave, man. You're **uglifying** my flat.* • *Tienes que irte, tío. Estás afeando mi piso.*

ungood *adj.*
Neologismo formado por el prefijo negativo **un** y el adjetivo **good**. Significa literalmente "desbueno", o sea, "malo".

—*Oh, no! A fail? This is so **ungood**.* • *¡Mierda! ¿Un suspenso? ¡Qué mal!*

ungoogleable *adj.*
INENCONTRABLE EN GOOGLE
Normalmente tiene el matiz de que es algo poco fiable.

—*I can't find any info on that company. Nothing's coming up on screen, they're **ungoogleable**.* • *No encuentro información sobre esa empresa; no sale nada en google.*

up against it *expr.*
JODIDO/A

—*We're **up against it** now. Sony and Samsung are in bed together.* • *Estamos jodidos. Sony y Samsung están haciendo negocios juntos.*

up on dat *expr.*
ENTERADO/A, AL DÍA

—*You gotta be **up on dat**.* • *Tienes que estar al día.*

upchuck *v.*
POTAR, ECHAR LA POTA

—*Out of my way! I'm gonna **upchuck**!* • *¡Apartaos, que voy a potar!*

upriver, upstate, up north *n.*
CHIRONA, TALEGO

—*Where's Johnny? Is he still **up north**?* • *¿Dónde está Johnny? ¿Sigue en chirona?*

vibe *n.*
VIBRACIONES, FEELING,
BUEN O MAL ROLLO

—*I get good vibes from Michael.* •
Michael me da buen feeling.

vomit comet [USA] *n.*
LÍNEA NOCTURNA DE AUTO-
BÚS URBANO, MAYORITARIA-
MENTE USADA POR BOLINGAS
POTANDO

—*Don't get a taxi, the vomit
comet'll be along in ten minutes.* •
*No pilles un taxi que el "bus de los
borrachos" pasa en diez minutos.*

veg out *v.*
VEGETAR

—*When I get off work, I just like
vegging out in front of the telly.* •
*Cuando salgo del curro, solo me
apetece vegetar delante de la tele.*

vpl *acron.*
(visible panty line)
SE MARCAN LAS BRAGAS

—*Look, lads! VPL.* • *¡Mirad chicos!
Se le marcan las bragas.*

verbal diarrhea *n.*
PAJAS MENTALES, CHORRADAS

—*That's just verbal diarrhea!* •
¡No me vengas con chorradas!

vet *n.*
VETERANO/A

—*"Born in the USA" is about a
troubled Vietnam vet.* • *"Born in
the USA" va de un veterano de la
guerra de Vietnam con problemas.*

volumes (speaks) *loc.*
DICE MUCHO

—*The look on her face speaks
volumes about what she feels about
you.* • *Su mirada dice mucho de lo
que siente por ti.*

WHAT DID HE SAY? // JUST THE USUAL, YADA YADA YADA • ¿QUÉ DIJO? // LO DE SIEMPRE: BLA, BLA, BLA

w00t! *expr.*
Esta es una expresión que indica victoria o júbilo en los juegos virtuales.

waffle *v.*
ENROLLARSE

—*Stop **waffling** and get to the point.* • No te enrolles y ve al grano.

wags *acron.*
(wives and girlfriends)
MUJERES Y NOVIAS

—*Newspaper headline: Capello Bans **WAGs** from England Training Camp.* • Titular de periódico: Capello prohíbe a las mujeres y novias de la selección inglesa asistir a la concentración.

waltz off with *v.*
MANGAR

—*Some wanker has **waltzed off with** my jacket.* • Algún cabrón me ha mangado la chaqueta.

wangle *v.*
CONSEGUIR ALGO CON ARTIMAÑAS

—*I'm gonna try and **wangle** an extra day's holiday.* • Voy a buscar la manera de que me den un día más de vacaciones.

wank *v., n.*
1 HACERSE UNA PAJA *(vul.)*

2 CHORRADA

—*Don't talk **wank**!* • ¡No digas chorradas!

3 wanker *n.*
CABRÓN, CAPULLO

—*Martha: He was seeing someone else. || Friend: **Wanker**!* • Martha: Estaba con otra. || Amiga: ¡Qué cabrón!

wannabe *n.*
UN/A QUIERO-Y-NO-PUEDO, UN/A IMITADOR/A

—*Kylie Minogue's just a **wannabe** Madonna.* • Kylie Minogue es una imitadora de Madonna.

Warhol moment n.
QUINCE MINUTOS DE GLORIA
O DE FAMA

—*Well, I got my **Warhol moment** this morning. They interviewed me for the telly.* • *Bueno, por fin he conseguido mis quince minutos de gloria esta mañana. Me han hecho una entrevista por la tele.*

wassup? expr. (what's up?)
¿QUÉ PASA?

—*Yo, dude! **Wassup?*** • *¿Qué pasa, tío?*

waste v.
ZURRAR, CALENTAR

—*I'm gonna **waste** you, weed!* • *¡Te voy a zurrar, mierdecilla!*

way interj.
ESO SÍ

—*No way! // Yeah, **way!*** • *¡Eso no! // ¡Sí, eso sí!*

wazz n.
MEADA, PIS

—*I was having a **wazz** in the street when the pigs arrived.* • *Estaba echando una meada en la calle cuando llegó la pasma.*

wazzed adj.
CIEGO/A, PEDO

—*What happened to you last night? You were **wazzed** after 3 drinks.* • *¿Qué te pasó ayer? Te pusiste ciega después de un par de copas.*

weed n.
1 DEBILUCHO, MIERDECILLA

—*Hey, shut up! **Weed!*** • *¡Oye tú, mierdecilla, cállate la boca!*

2 HIERBA, MARÍA

—*Get the **weed** out, man.* • *Saca la hierba, tío.*

wet ware n.
Término utilizado en mundos virtuales para referirse a los seres humanos en el mundo real.

whack v.
1 CARGARSE A ALGUIEN

—*They're gonna **whack** him.* • *Se lo van a cargar.*

2 whack off v. (vul.)
HACERSE UN PAJA, CASCÁRSELA

—*Dokes: I bet you **whack off** thinking about that shit. // Dexter: Me? Hell, no!* • *Dokes: Seguro que te la cascas pensando en esa mierda. // Dexter: ¿Yo? ¡Qué va!*

3 whacko adj.
LOCO/A, PIRADO/A

—*Don't talk to those guys. They're **whacko**.* • *No hables con esos tipos. Están piraos.*

what the hell *expr.*

QUÉ COJONES

—George: **What the hell** was that? // Dick: Dunno. • George: ¿Qué cojones ha sido eso? // Dick: Ni idea.

whatever *interj.*

YA VES, ME LA SUDA

—Husband: It's over between us. // Wife: Yeah, **whatever**. • Marido: Lo nuestro se ha acabado. // Mujer: Ya ves.

wheels *n.*

BUGA, CARRO

—Wanna see my new **wheels**? • ¿Quieres ver mi buga nuevo?

whistle for *v.*

ESPERAR SENTADO/A

—If you want it, you can **whistle for** it. • Si lo quieres, ya puedes esperar sentado.

whoop it up *v.*

PASARLO TETA

—Come along to the party and **whoop it up** all night long. • Ven a la fiesta y te lo pasarás teta, ya verás.

whopper *n.*

TROLA

—What a **whopper**! • ¡Vaya trola!

who's your daddy? *expr.*

¡TOMA YA!, ¡CHÚPATE ESA!

—After potting the black ball on the pool table: Yeeeees! **Who's your daddy**? • Después de meter la bola negra en una partida de billar: ¡Síííí! ¡Toma ya!

wicked *adj.*

GENIAL, BESTIAL

—Sophie: I got the job! // Manu: **Wicked**! • Sophie: ¡Me han dado el trabajo! // Manu: ¡Genial!

willy-nilly *adv.*

DE CUALQUIER MANERA

—You can't just come in and make comments like that, **willy-nilly**. • No puedes entrar así y hacer esos comentarios así de cualquier manera.

windbag *n.*

UN/A PLASTA, UN PESADO/A

—What a **windbag**! Always going on and on. • ¡Qué plasta el tío, cómo se enrolla!

wingman *n.*

ESCUDERO, ACOMPAÑANTE

—I'm going for the brunette. Wanna be my **wingman**? • Voy a ligar con la rubia. ¿Me acompañas?

wino *n.*

BORRACHO/A, ALCOHÓLICO/A

—*Graham: He was a great talent. Where is he now?* // *Kyle: He lost it. He's a* **wino** *now.* • *Graham: Era buenísimo. ¿Qué hace ahora?* // *Kyle: Lo perdió todo. Ahora es un borracho.*

wiped *adj.*

MOLIDO/A, FRITO/A

—*I'm gonna hit the sack. I'm* **wiped**. • *Me voy a la piltra. Estoy molido.*

wired *adj.*

HISTÉRICO/A, ATACADO/A

—*Don't say anything to her. She's* **wired**. • *No le digas nada. Está histérica.*

wobbler *n.*

MOSQUEO, CABREO

—*She threw a* **wobbler** *when she found out she didn't get the promotion.* • *Se pilló un buen cabreo cuando se enteró de que no le habían ascendido.*

woose, wuss *n.*

CAGUETA, GALLINA

—*Get in the water! Don't be a* **wuss**. • *¡Métete en el agua! No seas gallina.*

word is bond *expr.*

Esta expresión indica que lo que alguien dice es 100% verdad, que va a misa.

—*Dan: I don't believe him.* // *Gary: I do. His* **word is bond**. • *Dan: No le creo.* // *Gary: Yo sí. Lo que él dice va a misa.*

 **WORD UP!** *expr.*

CORRECTO, LA PURA VERDAD

—*Mark: Is that true?* // *Almu: Yeah,* **word up!** • *Mark: ¿Es verdad eso?* // *Almu: Sí, ¡la pura verdad!*

wow *acron.*
(world of warcraft)

—*Little brother: What does* **WoW** *mean?* // *Big brother: It means "World of Warcraft". Now, could you get out of my room, please?* • *Hermano pequeño: ¿Qué significa "WoW"?* // *Hermano mayor: "World of Warcraft". ¿Puedes largarte de mi habitación, por favor?*

wrecked *adj.*

PEDO, CIEGO/A

—*Duncan: Why did you say that?* // *Lindsay: Dunno, man. I was* **wrecked**. • *Duncan: ¿Por qué dijiste eso?* // *Lindsay: No lo sé, tío. Estaba pedo.*

wtf *acron.*
(what the fuck)

QUÉ COÑO

—*sms:* **WTF** *happened?* • *sms: ¿Qué coño pasó?*

yellow card *n., v.*

TARJETA AMARILLA
Expresa advertencia o desaproba-
ción, sobre todo cuando alguien
va en contra de la opinión general; como en el fútbol, en estos
casos se le saca "tarjeta amarilla".

—*Wilson: Right, lads! Let's go to a
club. // Johnson: No, I'm gonna call
it a day. // Lads: **Yellow card**, Johnson!* • *Wilson: ¡Venga, chicos! Vamos
a la disco. // Johnson: No, yo paso. //
¡Tarjeta amarilla, Johnson!*

yada yada yada *n.*

BLA BLA BLA

—*What did he say? // Just the usual,
yada yada yada.* • *¿Qué dijo? // Lo
de siempre: bla, bla, bla.*

yak *v.*

POTAR

—*Open the window, please. I'm
gonna **yak**!* • *Abre la ventana, por
favor, que voy a potar.*

yeah right *interj.*

ANDA YA, SÍ, HOMBRE

—*Lads: Look, Pete! Your idol's just
walked in the door. // Pete: **Yeah,
right!*** • *Los colegas: Pete, mira
quien entra por la puerta: tu ídolo. //
Pete: ¡Anda ya!*

yo *interj.*

¡QUÉ PASA!

—***Yo**, dude!* • *¡Qué pasa, tío!*

you and your mama *interj.*

NI DE COÑA, ANDA YA,
SÍ, HOMBRE, TÚ Y QUIÉN MÁS

—*I'm gonna deck you! // Yeah, **you
and your mama**.* • *¡Te voy a pegar
una hostia! // ¡Sí, hombre!*

yuk *interj.*

PUAJ, QUÉ ASCO

—*Spinach! **Yuk**!* • *¡Espinacas! ¡Puaj!*

yummy *adj., interj.*

DELICIOSO/A, PARA CHUPARSE
LOS DEDOS, PARA MOJAR PAN Y
NO PARAR

—*Chocolate cake! **Yummy**!* • *¡Tar-
ta de chocolate! ¡Mmm!*

zap into *v.*

ENTRAR UN MOMENTO EN UN LUGAR, ESPECIALMENTE CUANDO ESTÁS DE COMPRAS

—*Stay here, please. I'm just gonna* ***zap into*** *the super for some bread and milk.* • *Quédate aquí, por favor. Voy un segundo al súper a por leche y pan.*

zero hour *n.*

HORA QUE INDICA EL INICIO DE ALGO

—*OK, everybody. An early start tomorrow.* ***Zero hour*** *07:00.* • *Atención todo el mundo. Mañana empezamos pronto. Hora de inicio, las 7 de la mañana.*

zero tolerance *n.*

TOLERANCIA CERO

—*Slogan:* ***Zero tolerance*** *against wife beaters.* • *Eslogan: Contra el maltratador, tolerancia cero.*

zilch *n.*

NADA DE NADA, CERO PATATERO

—*So, what did you get from the inheritance?* || ***Zilch!*** • *¿Entonces, qué te tocó de herencia?* || *¡Nada, cero patatero!*

zit *n.*

GRANO, ESPINILLA

—*Hey! You've got a* ***zit*** *on your nose.* • *¡Oye! Tienes un grano en la nariz.*

2 pop a zit *loc.*

REVENTAR UN GRANO

—*That's a gross zit you got, Johnny. Pop it, man!* • *Es muy asqueroso este grano que te ha salido, Johnny. ¡Reviéntalo ya!*

zonked *adj.*

SOBADO, FRITO/ A

—*Hey! Wake up!* || *Just leave him. He's* ***zonked.*** • *¡Eh, tú! ¡Despierta!* || *Déjale, que está sobao.*

ESPAÑOL-ENGLISH

abrirse _v. prnl._

TO SHOOT OFF, TO HIT THE
ROAD, TO HIT THE DOOR

—_¡Vaya bodrio de fiesta, yo me **abro**!_ • _What a shit party! I'm gonna hit the road!_

acojonar _v._

1 TO FREAK OUT

—_¡Menudo antro! Yo me abro, este lugar me **acojona**!_ • _What a dive! I'm out of here, this place freaks me out._

2 acojonarse _v. prnl._

TO CHICKEN OUT, TO BACK
DOWN, TO GET COLD FEET

—_Mario se ha vuelto a **acojonar**._ • _Mario chickened out again._

3 acojonado/a (estar) _adj._

TO BE SCARED SHITLESS,
TO BE FREAKED OUT

—_¡Estoy **acojonada**! Me han llamado de Hacienda._ • _I'm scared shitless! I got a call from the tax man._

Cojones are balls of the man kind. Just as we do in English, Spanish takes these balls and turns them into verbs, adjectives and adverbs. As you may see the effect is rather similar, but then again, a little different.

4 acojonante _adj._

SLICK, SEXCELLENT, ACE

—_Este móvil es **acojonante**, tiene mogollón de funciones._ • _This mobile's so slick, it's got a shitload of functions._

adicto/a (ser) _loc._

TO BE HOOKED

—_Mark es **adicto** al facebook._ • _Mark's hooked on facebook._

agarrado/a _adj._

STINGY, CHEAPSKATE,
TIGHT-FISTED

—_Espero que no venga el **agarrado** de tu hermano, no hay manera de que afloje la pasta para nada._ • _I hope your stingy brother doesn't come, you just can't get any dough out of him._

agenciarse v. prnl.

TO WALTZ OFF WITH, TO NICK.

—No te **agencies** ese boli que es mío, tío. • Don't even think about waltzing off with that pen, mate. It's mine.

agobiar v.

1 TO PRESSURE SOMEBODY

—¡No me **agobies**, tío! • Don't pressure me, pal!

2 agobiarse v. prnl.

TO WORRY

—Laura **se agobia** enseguida. • Laura worries at the slightest thing.

agonías adj., n.

A MOANER, A MOANING GIT

—¡Vaya **agonías** que estás hecho! Siempre te estás quejando de algo. • You moaning git! You're always going on about something!

alerón n.

PIT (ARMPIT)

—¡Cómo te canta el **alerón**, colega! • Your pits are minging, mate!

alucinar v.

TO BE GOBSMACKED

This originally only referred to being spaced out on drugs, but these days you can be **alucinado/a** by anything but drugs. This word has gone mainstream.

—Yo **alucino** en colores contigo tía, vaya bronca que le has echado. • I'm gobsmacked, you really bawled him out.

amañado/a adj.

RIGGED, FIXED

—El partido estaba claramente **amañado**. • The match was clearly rigged.

¡anda ya! expr.

In Spanish, if you really want to express that you don't agree at all, gain the upper hand by showing your superior knowledge and belittle the person you're talking to – then all you need to say is, **¡Anda ya!** or **¡Sí, hombre!**

antro n.

A DIVE, A DUMP

—Menudo **antro**, yo me abro. • What a dive. I'm outta here.

apalancarse v. prnl.

TO SLOB AROUND, TO VEG OUT

—Venga tío, no te **apalanques** en el sofá, que vamos a llegar a la fiesta a las mil. • Come on, mate! Stop slobbing around, we're never gonna get there on time.

apañárselas *v. prnl.*

1 TO GET BY, TIDE (SOMEONE) OVER, TO MANAGE

—*Ya que no me necesitas, **te las apañas** tú solito a partir de ahora.* • *You don't need me anymore, you can get by on your own from now on.*

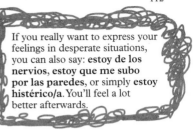

If you really want to express your feelings in desperate situations, you can also say: **estoy de los nervios, estoy que me subo por las paredes,** or simply **estoy histérico/a.** You'll feel a lot better afterwards.

2 apañado/a *adj.*
A JACK-OF-ALL TRADES, HANDY

—*Hija, qué **apañada**, sabes hacer de todo.* • *Wow, you're a jack-of-all-trades, you can do anything.*

apoquinar *v.*

TO FORK OUT, TO SPLASH OUT

—*¿Cuánto toca **apoquinar** a cada uno? ¿10 euros?* • *How much do we fork out each? 10 Euros?*

arrastre (estar para el) *loc.*

TO BE SHAGGED OUT, TO BE KNACKERED

—*¿Salir esta noche? ¡Ni de coña! **Estoy para el arrastre.*** • *Out tonight? No way! I'm shagged out.*

atacado/a *adj.*

FREAKED OUT, WIRED

—*Estoy **atacada**, mañana expongo mi tesis ante el tribunal.* • *I'm freaked out, I'm presenting my thesis to the panel tomorrow.*

atiborrarse *v. prnl.*

TO PIG OUT ON

—*Nos hemos **atiborrado** de patatas fritas y ahora no me apetece comer.* • *We've pigged out on chips and I can't eat lunch now.*

YOU CAN ALSO SAY PONERSE MORADO/A OR COMER COMO UN/A CERDO/A...

atravesado/a (tener algo o a alguien) *loc.*

TO NOT GET ON, TO GO OR GET NOWHERE

—*¡Qué horror! Esta asignatura la tengo **atravesada**. Me van a catear otra vez.* • *Oh, man! I'm getting nowhere with this subject. I'm gonna flunk it again.*

atufar *v.*

TO MING, TO PONG

—*Abrid una ventana por favor, aquí **atufa** a tigre.* • *Open a window, it's minging in here.*

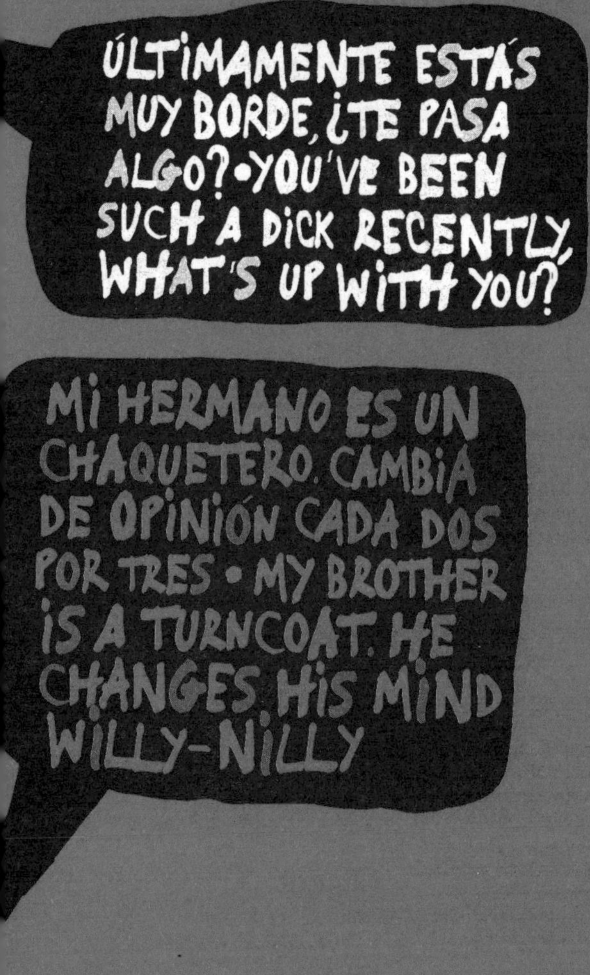
ÚLTIMAMENTE ESTÁS MUY BORDE, ¿TE PASA ALGO? • YOU'VE BEEN SUCH A DICK RECENTLY, WHAT'S UP WITH YOU?
MI HERMANO ES UN CHAQUETERO. CAMBIA DE OPINIÓN CADA DOS POR TRES • MY BROTHER IS A TURNCOAT. HE CHANGES HIS MIND WILLY-NILLY

baboso/a *adj.*
WORM

—*Ese tío es muy **baboso**. Se pasa el día hablando de mujeres, que si esa está buenísima, que si la otra es un pibón...* • *That guy's a worm. He goes on and on talking about chicks, she's hot, the other one's a babe...*

bajón *n.*
COMEDOWN, TO BE ON A DOWNER
After using drugs the **bajón** is that big comedown. It's also a big depression caused by life in general. The opposite is the **subidón**.

—*Tenemos que animar a Raquel que está de **bajón**, le han vuelto a suspender el examen.* • *We've got to cheer Raquel up, she's on a right downer, she's failed her driving test again.*

baldado/a *adj.*
KNACKERED, SHATTERED,

—*¡Qué paliza nos ha metido el entrenador, estoy **baldao**!* • *The trainer gave us a right work out, I'm knackered.*

bareto *n.*
BOOZER

—*Esta zona está llena de **baretos** guays.* • *This place is full of great boozers.*

bartola (tumbarse a la) *loc.*
TO VEG OUT, TO SCRATCH ONE'S BALLS, TO DO EFF ALL

—*Los domingos me encanta **tumbarme a la bartola**.* • *I love vegging out on Sundays.*

berenjenal (meterse en un) *loc.*
TO BE IN DEEP SHIT

—*En buen **berenjenal** nos hemos metido.* • *We're really in deep shit now.*

YOU CAN ALSO SAY METERSE EN UN JARDÍN

bestial *adj.*
ACE

—*¡Es **bestial** que te hayan dado ese premio!* • *That's ace that you got the prize!*

birra *n.*

AN ICE COLD (BEER)

—¿Me pasas una **birra** de la nevera? • Can you get me an ice cold from the kegerator?

blanco (quedarse en) *loc.*

TO HAVE A BRAIN FART

—**Me quedé** totalmente **en blanco** en el examen de Filo. ¡Qué putada! • I had a total brain fart in the philosophy exam. What a bummer!

bocas *n.*

1 GOBSHITE, BIG MOUTH

—Jaime es un **bocas**, el tío habla mucho, se las da de listo, pero en el fondo no sabe de la misa la mitad. • Jaime's such a gobshite, the guy really talks, plays the smartass, but deep down he doesn`t know shit.

2 RAT, GRASS

—¡Menudo **bocas** tu hermano! Ya lo ha largado todo. • What a grass your brother is! He totally ratted out on us.

bodrio *n.*

Again in English an adjective is needed to express our feelings over something which is so boring or so crap it's piss poor.

—La fiesta del viernes fue un **bodrio**, nos aburrimos mogollón. • Friday's party was so piss poor, we were bored shitless.

bola *n.*

1 A WHOPPER, TOTAL PORKIES

—Todo lo que cuentas son **bolas**. • You just tell total porkies.

UNA TROLA IS THE SAME THING AS UNA BOLA. IN BOTH CASES, YOU ARE TALKING OUT YOUR ASS

2 bolas (en) *loc.*

STARKERS, IN THE BUFF

—El capullo se quedó **en bolas** delante de todo el mundo. • The prick was starkers in front of everybody.

EN BOLAS, EN PELOTAS OR EN CUEROS ARE DIFFERENT WAYS TO SAY THAT YOU ARE IN YOUR BIRTHDAY SUIT

bollera, bollo *n.*

DYKE

—No entiendo por qué no sale del armario de una vez. Si todo el mundo sabe que es **bollera**. • I don't get why she just doesn't just come out of the closet. Everybody knows she's a dyke.

bollicao *n.*

TOY BOY

—Marta siempre sale con **bollicaos**. • Marta's always got a toy boy.

bomba (pasarlo) *loc.*

TO HAVE A BALL

—*Nos **lo pasamos bomba** en la fiesta del sábado.* • *We had a ball at the party last Saturday.*

borde *adj., n.*

A DICK, DICKHEAD, ASSHOLE

—*Últimamente estás muy **borde**, ¿te pasa algo?* • *You've been such a dick recently, what's up with you?*

botas (ponerse las) *loc.*

TO PIG OUT

—*El sábado **nos pusimos las botas** en casa de Elena y Tom, comimos hasta reventar.* • *We went to Elena and Tom's on Saturday and just pigged out.*

IT DOESN'T JUST MEAN FOOD. YOU CAN PONERTE LAS BOTAS WITH ANYTHING IN SPANISH

bote *n.*

1 KITTY

—*Hay que poner 5 euros de **bote** para el botellón.* • *You've to put 5 Euros in the kitty for the carry out.*

2 a bote pronto *loc.*

OFF THE TOP OF MY HEAD

—*¿Qué cuál es mi grupo favorito? Hombre, así **a bote pronto** diría Coldplay.* • *What's my favourite group? Off the top of my head, I'd say Coldplay.*

3 rubia de bote *loc.*

BOTTLE BLONDE

—*Jessica es **rubia de bote**. No te creas que es sueca.* • *Jessica is a bottle blonde. Don't go thinking she's Swedish.*

4 en el bote *loc.*

IN THE BAG, EATING OUT OF ONE'S HAND

—*Ve a hablar con él, lo tienes en el **bote**.* • *Go up and speak to him, you've got him in the bag.*

botellón *n.*

Friends gathering behind the cornershop, in an out-of-the-way place or even in full view with a humungous carry out containing the cheapest, nastiest booze that their scarce funds can afford. Does that ring a bell? Well, it's part of Spanish culture too. This used to happen in the **plazas** (squares) of towns and cities until the government outlawed it and sent the fuzz in to enforce it. But, it still goes on in those out-of-the-way places now.

—*Esta noche hacemos **botellón** en la playa.* • *We're having a piss-up on the beach tonight.*

braguetazo *n.*

GOLD DIGGER

—*Menudo **braguetazo** el de Tony,*

se va a casar con esa empresaria vieja que está forrada. • *Tony's a total gold digger. He's gonna marry that old, minted business woman.*

brasa (dar la) *loc.*

1 TO BUG, TO BE A PAIN

2 brasas *n.*

WINDBAG

—*Ten cuidado con ese tío que es un **brasas**, ni te acerques.* // *¡Ya, ya!, ya he visto cómo **le daba la brasa** a la pobre Mariluz.* • *¡Watch out. That guy's a windbag, stay clear.* // *Yeah, yeah. I saw how he was bugging Mariluz.*

bronca(s) *n.*

1 DING-DONG

—*Anoche los vecinos montaron una buena **bronca**.* • *There was a right ding-dong with the neighbours last night.*

2 broncas

WANKER, SCUMBAG

—*Ya me lo puedo imaginar, es un **broncas** de mucho cuidado, siempre la está montando.* • *Tell me about it, he's a right wanker, he's always at it.*

brutal *adj.*

ACE

—*El botellón será **brutal**, viene todo Dios.* • *The piss-up will be ace, everyone and his dog is coming.*

buenorro/a *adj.*

HOT

—*¡Ese tío está super**buenorro**!* • *That guy's really hot!*

buitre *n.*

SCROUNGER, MOOCHER

—*A Tony no lo invites que es un **buitre**.* • *Don't invite Tony, he's a scrounger.*

bujarra(s) *n. (vul.)*

POOF

—*El profe de inglés es **bujarras** fijo. Tiene mucha pluma.* • *The English teacher's a total poof. He's as camp as a row of frilly tents.*

bulla *n.*

DING DONG, RACKET

—*Se armó una buena **bulla** en el curro.* • *There was a right ding dong at work.*

burra *n.*

SCOOTER

—*Me he pegado una leche con la **burra**.* • *I gave the scooter a right bang.*

burrada *n.*

PORKIES, TALL STORIES

—*No dices más que **burradas**.* • *You tell nothing but porkies.*

caballo *n.*

SMACK

—*Ese camello solo pasa* **caballo**. •
That d-boy only deals smack.

cabeza (estar mal de la) *loc.*

TO BE OFF ONE'S ROCKER,
TO BE NUTS, TO BE MENTAL

—*¿De qué vas? ¡Pasa de mí, tú*
estás mal de la cabeza! • *What's*
your game? Leave me alone, you're
off your rocker!

cable

1 cruzársele los cables *loc.*

TO LOSE THE PLACE TOTALLY,
TO GO MAD

—*Se le cruzaron los cables y nos*
echó de su casa. • *He totally lost the*
place and kicked us out.

2 echar un cable *loc.*

TO LEND A HAND

—*¡Échame un cable con estos*
papeles, por favor! No capisco nada.
• *Lend me a hand with these papers,*
will you? I just don't get it.

cabra (estar como una) *loc.*

TO BE MENTAL, TO BE NUTS,
TO BE OFF ONE'S ROCKER

—*Blanca está como una cabra,*
nos lo pasamos genial con ella. •
Blanca's mental. We had a great
laugh with her.

cabrearse *v. prnl.*

1 TO GET PISSED OFF, TO GET HACKED OFF

—*Mi hermana se ha cabreado*
conmigo por una chorrada. • *My*
sister got pissed off with me for
nothing.

2 cabreado/a *adj.*

PISSED OFF

—*Déjame, que estoy muy cabrea-*
da. • *Leave me alone, I'm really*
pissed off.

3 cabreo *n.*

STATE OF BEING PISSED OFF

—*¡Vaya cabreo que se agarró tu*
padre el otro día! • *Your dad got*
really pissed off the other day!

cabrón/a *n., adj.*

1 WANKER

—*Mi jefe es un **cabrón**. Le encanta putear a la gente.* • *My boss is a right wanker. He loves fucking people over.*

2 SON OF A BITCH (BUT IN A GUY TO GUY GOOD WAY)

—*¡Qué **cabrón**! Al final se ha salido con la suya.* • *You son of a bitch! You got your own way in the end.*

cacao *n.*

FUZZY MATH(S)

—*Cuanto más estudio, más **cacao** tengo en el coco.* • *The more I study, the more the fuzzy maths fills my nut.*

cachas *adj.*

HUNK

—*Claro que está **cachas**, se pasa la vida en el gimnasio.* • *Of course he's a hunk, he spends all day in the gym.*

cacho (un) *n.*

1 A BIT

—*Dame **un cacho** de esto que estás comiendo.* • *Gimme a bit of what you're eating.*

2 pillar cacho *loc.*

TO GET SOME ACTION

—*Anoche fue un desastre, no **pillamos cacho**.* • *Last night was a disaster, we didn't get any action.*

cachondearse *v. prnl.*

1 TO TAKE THE PISS, TO TAKE THE MICKEY

—*A Mario le encanta **cachondearse** de todo el mundo.* • *Mario loves taking the piss out of everybody.*

2 cachondeo *n.*

PISS TAKING

—*En la clase siempre hay mucho **cachondeo**.* • *There's a lot of piss taking in class.*

cachondo/a *adj.*

1 HORNY

—*Esta churry me pone **cachondo**.* • *This chick makes me horny.*

2 A GOOD LAUGH

—*Blanca es una **cachonda** mental.* • *Blanca's a real good laugh.*

cagada *n.*

A BALLS UP, A FUCK UP

—*Vaya **cagada** la que acabo de hacer en el trabajo.* • *What a balls up at work.*

cagadero *n.*

THE SHITTER, THE BOG, THE JOHN

—*¡Joder! Los **cagaderos** de este antro están siempre supersucios.* • *Fuck's sake! The bogs in this dive are always filthy.*

cagado/a *adj.*

TO SHIT ONESELF

—*Estoy cagada, tía, el jefe me ha dicho que vaya a verlo.* • *Oh, man, I'm shitting myself. The boss has asked to see me.*

cagalera *n.*

TO HAVE THE SHITTERS

—*¡Sal del baño, me ha entrado cagalera!* • *Get out of the bog! I've got the shitters!*

cagarse *v. prnl.*

1 TO SHIT ONESELF

—*Te vas a cagar cuando se entere el jefe.* • *You're gonna shit yourself when the boss finds out.*

2 cagarla *v.*

TO BALLS UP, TO FUCK UP, TO BLOW IT

—*La he cagado en ese proyecto.* • *I've ballsed this project up.*

3 cagarse de frío *loc.*

TO BE FUCKING COLD

—*Cierra la ventana, nos cagamos de frío.* • *Shut the window ,we're fucking cold.*

4 cagarse de miedo *loc.*

TO SHIT ONESELF, TO BE SHIT SCARED

—*Vaya broma más estupida. ¡Me he cagado de miedo, gilipollas!* • *What a stupid prank. I shat myself. You prick!*

5 cagarse en alguien *loc.*

FUCK THEM

In Spanish , if you're really pissed off with somebody, you say that "I shit on them". Obviously we can't say that in English, although it's rather funny.

—*Mi jefe me ha dicho que tenía mentalidad de funcionario. ¡Me cago en este gilipollas!* • *My boss said I've got a civil servant's mentality. Fuck him!*

6 cagarse en todo *loc.*

You can also "shit on everything" in Spanish although in English we prefer to say "fuck", "fuck it" or "fuck them all".

—*Me han robado en mi propia casa. Me cago en todo.* • *They burgled my house. Fuck them all.*

calada *n.*

A TOKE, A DRAG, A DRAW

—*Pásame una calada que no quiero fumar uno entero.* • *Gimme a toke, I don't wanna smoke it all.*

caldo (poner a) *loc.*

TO PAN, TO SLAG OFF

—*Te pusieron a caldo en la reunión.* • *You got panned at the meeting.*

ALSO: PONER DE VUELTA Y MEDIA, PONER VERDE...

calentón n.

A DOSE OF THE HORN

—*Esa tía simplemente se cachondeó de mí y yo me fui a casa con un buen **calentón**.* • *That bird was just having me on and I went home with a dose of the horn.*

calentorro/a n.

A HORNY GIT

—*Carlos es un **calentorro**. Solo piensa en follar.* • *Carlos is a horny git. He's always thinking about getting his end away.*

calientabraguetas, calientapollas n. (vul.)

COCKTEASE

—*No te flipes, es solo una **calientabraguetas**.* • *Chillax, she's just a cocktease.*

calimocho n.

Red wine and coke. Yeah, really! A traditional drink among those young and recently initiated drinkers.

—*En la uni no teníamos mucha pasta, así que nos poníamos ciegos a **calimocho**.* • *At uni we never had much money, so we used to get hammered on red wine and coke.*

callejear v.

TO WANDER THE STREETS

—*Ayer estuvimos **callejeando** por Barcelona y nos encantó.* • *We were wandering the Barcelona streets yesterday and we loved it.*

callo n.

1 A MINGER, A DOG, A FUGLY BIRD/CHICK OR BLOKE/GUY

—*Beatriz dice que aquí solo hay **callos**, no entremos.* • *Beatriz says this place is full of mingers, we're not going in.*

2 dar el callo loc.

TO SLOG, TO GRIND

—*Aquí nadie **da el callo**, ¡vaya panda de vagos!* • *Nobody wants to slog here. What a bunch of lazy bastards!*

calvo (hacer un) loc.

TO MOON, TO SHOW ONE'S ARSE

—*Jordi siempre acaba la noche **haciendo calvos**.* • *Jordi always ends the night mooning.*

calzonazos n.

A HENPECKED MAN, A YES-MAN

—*El marido de Carmen es un **calzonazos**.* • *Carmen's man's henpecked.*

camelar v.

1 TO HIT ON SOMEBODY

—*¿Me estás **camelando**?* • *Are you hitting on me?*

2 TO TALK SOMEBODY INTO SOMETHING

—*Al final el vendedor me acabó **camelando** y compré esa cafetera de George Clooney.* • *In the end the rep talked me into it and I bought this George Clooney coffee maker.*

camello *n.*

DEALER

—*Ese **camello** solo pasa costo.* • *That dealer only does hash.*

canutas (pasarlas) *loc.*

TO HAVE A HARD TIME

—*En la posguerra mis abuelos **las pasaron canutas**.* • *After the war my grandparents had a hard time.*

canuto *n.*

A JOINT

—*Este **canuto** está supercargado, tío.* • *This joint's mega strong, dude.*

THERE ARE SHITLOADS OF WORDS FOR JOINT IN SPANISH, JUST LIKE IN ENGLISH. IF YOU'RE INTO SMOKING CULTURE, GET YOUR SYNONYMS READY AND BE PREPARED TO ASK SOMEBODY TO PASS THE PETA, PORRO, CANUTO OR FLY...

cantar *v.*

1 TO GRASS, TO FINK OUT

—*Al final el detenido acabó **cantando**.* • *The accused ended up finking out.*

2 cantar las cuarenta *loc.*

TO LAY INTO SOMEBODY

—*Mi madre me **cantó las cuarenta** por llegar tarde.* • *My mum really laid into me for getting home late.*

caña *n.*

1 A LITTLE BEER

Unlike English-speaking culture, the most popular way to drink beer is to have a little one, i.e. the **caña** which is normally accompanied by a **tapa**, meaning snack. So, you can be macho when you get back home, for now enjoy the caña culture.

—*Invítame a una **caña**, tío.* • *Get me a beer, mate.*

2 meter caña *loc.*

TO GIVE IT SOME, TO BOMB

—*¡Venga tío! ¡Métele **caña**!* • *Come on, mate! Give it some!*

cañero/a *adj.*

JUMPING (GOOD ATMOSPHERE)

—*Este garito es muy **cañero**.* • *This boozer's jumping.*

cañón *adj.*

HOT

—*La novia de Paul está **cañón**.* • *Paul's bird's hot.*

capullo/a *n.*

A WANKER

—*El amigo de Ramón es un **capullo**.* • *Ramon's mate's a right wanker.*

carca *n., adj.*

OLD SCHOOL

—*Mi padre es un **carca**.* • *My dad's so old school.*

cardo *n.*

A MINGER, A DOG, A FUGLY BIRD/CHICK OR BLOKE/GUY

—*Ese tío me ha llamado **cardo**, ¡será capullo!* • *That guy called me fugly. What a wanker!*

THE EXTENDED VERSION OF THIS INSULT IS CARDO BORRIQUERO

cargarse *v. prnl.*

1 TO WHACK

—*Se han **cargado** a un capo de la Mafia.* • *They whacked the Mafia boss.*

2 TO BREAK

—*¿Quién se ha **cargado** la mesa?* • *Who broke the table?*

3 cargárselas

TO CARRY THE CAN

—*Siempre me las acabo **cargando** yo. ¡Estoy harto!* • *I always end up carrying the can. I'm pissed off!*

cascado/a *adj.*

TO BE LONG IN THE TOOTH

—*Antonio está ya muy **cascado** para seguir el ritmo que lleva.* • *Antonio's a bit long in the tooth to be doing what he's doing.*

cascársela *v. prnl. (vul.)*

TO HAVE A WANK

catear *v.*

TO FLUNK AN EXAM

—*Me van a matar en casa, ¡he vuelto a **catearlo** todo!* • *I'm dead, I've flunked them all again!*

cateto/a *n.*

LOUT

—*No tienes ni idea de nada, eres un **cateto**.* • *You haven't got a clue, you lout.*

catre *n.*

PIT, SACK (BED)

—*Estoy hecha polvo, me voy al **catre**.*

• *I'm knackered, I'm going to hit the sack.*

cegato/a *adj.*

BLIND AS A BAT

—*Almu debería ir al oculista porque está **cegata** perdida.* • *Almu should go to the optician's, she's as blind as a bat.*

cepillarse *v. prnl.*

1 TO WHACK (KILL)

—**Se han cepillado** *al jefe de la mafia.* • *The Mafia boss got whacked.*

2 TO SHAG

—*Ese tío **se cepilla** todo lo que se mueve.* • *That guy shags anything that moves.*

cháchara (estar de) *loc.*

TO CHEW THE FAT

—*Anoche **estuvimos de cháchara** hasta las tantas.* • *We chewed the fat till who knows what time last night.*

chalado/a *adj.*

MENTAL, BONKERS

—*Salir a pasear con la que está cayendo es de **chalados**.* • *Going out in that rain's just mental.*

chapar *v.*

TO SHUT

—*A esta hora está todo **chapado** en este pueblo.* • *At this time everything's shut in this town.*

chapucero/a *adj.*

1 A FUCK UP, A BOTCH UP

—*Ya he entregado el trabajo de Física. Me ha quedado **chapucero**.* • *I handed my Physics essay in. It was a fuck up.*

2 chapuza *n.*

A BOTCH UP, A FUCK UP

—*Los paletas me han hecho una **chapuza** en casa que mejor ni te cuento. Estoy desesperada.* • *The workies left a total botch up at home, don't even talk to me about it. I don't know what to do.*

chaquetero/a *n., adj.*

A TURNCOAT

—*Mi hermano es un **chaquetero**. Cambia de opinión cada dos por tres.* • *My brother is a turncoat. He changes his mind willly-nilly.*

chatear *v.*

TO CHAT

—*Mari Carmen se pasa todo el día **chateando**.* • *Mari Carmen spends all day chatting.*

chati *n.*

BABE, CHICK, BIRD

—*Pedro y yo hemos quedado con dos **chatis** que conocimos en la disco el finde pasado.* • *Pedro and I are meeting up with those chicks we met at the disco last weekend.*

CHURRI CAN REFER TO A LASS IN GENERAL OR TO ONE'S GIRLFRIEND, A CHATI HOWEVER IS NEVER A GIRLFRIEND

china *n.*

A BLOCK OF HASH

—*He perdido la **china** por el camino.* • *I lost my block of hash on the way.*

chiringuito *n.*

A BEACH BAR

—*Ayer estuvimos en los **chiringuitos** de la Barceloneta.* • *We were at the beach bars in Barceloneta yesterday.*

chiripa (de) *loc.*

FLUKE

—*Marcó un gol **de chiripa**.* • *He scored a fluke goal.*

chirona *n.*

THE NICK, THE SLAMMER

—*Lo metieron en **chirona** por pasar costo delante del insti.* • *They stuck him in the nick for doing hash in front of the school.*

chisme *n.*

1 THINGY, THINGUMMYJIG

—*Pásame ese **chisme** para cortar.* • *Pass me the thingummyjig for cutting the thingy.*

2 THE GOSS (GOSSIP)

—*¿Has oido los **chismes** que cuentan de Lola?* • *Have you heard the goss they're spreading about Lola?*

chivarse *v. prnl.*

1 TO GRASS ON SOMEBODY, TO RAT ON SOMEBODY

—*Fue mi hermano el que se **chivó** a mi madre del ciego del sábado.* • *It was my brother who ratted on me to my ma about the piss-up on Saturday.*

2 chivato/a *n.*

A RAT, GRASS, FINK

—*¡Menudo **chivato** tu hermano!* • *What a fink, your bro'!*

chochear *v.*

TO LOSE ONE'S MENTAL ABILITIES DUE TO AGE, TO SHOW SIGNS OF DEMENTIA

—*No sé que te pasa pero última-*

mente **chocheas** *mucho.* • *I don't know what's up but recently you've been showing signs of dementia.*

cholo/a *n.*

CHAV

—*¡Joder tío casi me zurro con un* **cholo** *en ese garito!* • *Fuck's sake, man! I almost got into a fight with a chav down the boozer.*

chorbo/a *n.*

LAD, BLOKE, GUY OR LASS, BIRD

—*Blanca aún conserva su* **chorbo-agenda.** • *Blanca still keeps her guy-diary.*

chorizar *v.*

1 TO NICK, TO GANK

—*Me han intentado* **chorizar** *el bolso en el metro.* • *Somebody tried to nick my bag on the underground*

2 chorizo/a *n.*

THIEF

—*Tienes que tener mucho cuidado porque Las Ramblas están llenas de* **chorizos.** • *Be very careful down the Ramblas, it's full of thieves.*

Besides **chorizar**, you can **mangar** or **chorrear** anything. Just be careful you don't get caught, though.

chorrada *n.*

BULLSHIT, CRAP

—*¡No dices más que* **chorradas,** *calla un poco!* • *You're talking bullshit.Why don't you shut it?*

chuches *n. pl.*

SWEETIES

—*De tanto comer* **chuches** *a tu hijo se le van a podrir los dientes.* • *Eating so many sweeties will rot your kid's teeth.*

chucho *n.*

MUTT (DOG)

—*¿Te gustan los* **chuchos?** • *Do you like mutts?*

chulo/a *adj., n.*

1 COOL, ACE

—*Me flipa tu chupa , es súper* **chula.** • *I dig the jacket, it's mega cool.*

2 FLASH

—*No me mola el novio de Blanca, es un poco* **chulo.** • *I don't dig Blanca's new man, he's a bit flash.*

3 A PIMP

—*La verdad es que parece su* **chulo.** • *The truth is he looks like her pimp.*

chumba chumba *n.*

HARDCORE DANCE MUSIC

—*Vamos al garito de la esquina que tiene buena pinta.* // *Yo paso que es* de **chumba chumba** y no me mola nada. • Let's go to that boozer on the corner, it looks cool. // Nah, I'm not into it, it's a hardcore dance place and I can't stand that.

chungo/a *adj.*

1 DODGY, IFFY, GAMMY

—Ese tío es un **chungo**, siempre está metido en todos los líos. • That guy's dodgy, he always gets involved in the argy-bargy.

2 HEAVY (DIFFICULT)

—La situación la veo un poco **chunga**. • This is a heavy situation.

3 DODGY (SICK, ILL)

—Laura no ha ido a trabajar porque estaba un poco **chunga**. • Laura didn't come to work today 'cos she's a bit dodgy.

chupado/a *adj.*

EASY-PEASY, CAKE

—El examen de Química estaba **chupado**. Toda la clase aprobó. • The Chemistry exam was easy-peasy. The whole class passed.

chupetón *n.*

HICKEY, NOOKIE BADGE, LOVE BITE

—¡Vaya **chupetón** que llevas en el cuello! ¡Ponte un pañuelo! • What a hickey you've got on your neck! Put a scarf on!

chupito *n.*

A SHOT (BOOZE)

—Creo que anoche nos pasamos un poco con los **chupitos**. • I think we did too many shots last night.

churri *n.*

CHICK, BIRD

—Voy a pegarle una torta a este quillo si sigue mirando a mi **churri**. • I'm gonna deck that chav if he keeps eyeing up my chick.

CHURRI CAN REFER TO A CHICK OR LASS IN GENERAL OR TO ONE'S GIRLFRIEND

churro/a *n.*

A FUCK UP, A BALLS UP

—No puedo presentar este dibujo, me ha salido un **churro**. • I can't hand in this drawing, it's turned out to be a right fuck up.

chusma *n.*

RIFF-RAFF, RABBLE

—¡Ese pavo es **chusma**! Ni te acerques. • He's just riff-raff! Stay well away.

ciego/a *adj., n.*

PISSED [UK] , WELLIED, WAZZED, HAMMERED, BLOTTO

—Creo que todos íbamos muy **ciegos** el sábado. • I think we were all wellied on Saturday.

cien (poner a) *loc.*

TO GIVE SOMEONE THE HORN

—Elena me **pone a cien**. • Elena gives me the horn.

clavada *n.*

A RIP OFF

—No vayas a ese restaurante porque siempre nos meten una **clavada** que te cagas. • Don't go to that restaurant, the prices are a total rip off.

cobrar *v.*

TO GET DECKED

—¡Laurita como sigas así vas a **cobrar**! • Laurita, if you carry on like that, you're gonna get decked!

cocer *v.*

TO BE UP TO SOMETHING

—No sé que hablan esos dos, pero algo están **cociendo**. • I don't

know what they're talking about, but they're up to something.

THE STANDARD VERB FOR THIS IS TRAMAR

coco *n.*

1 NUT, NOGGIN

—¡Me va estallar el **coco**! • My nut's gonna burst!

2 comerse el coco *loc.*

TO HAVE A HAMSTER WHEEL BRAIN

—No te **comas el coco** por lo de la comida. Iremos a comer un bocadillo. • Get rid of the hamster wheel brain about lunch. We'll have just sandwiches.

cojones *n.*

1 estar hasta los cojones *loc.*

TO BE UP TO HERE

—Andrés **está hasta los cojones** de su madre, se va a independizar en cuanto pueda. • Andres is up to here with his mum. He's leaving home asap.

2 tocar los cojones *loc.*

TO PISS SOMEBODY OFF

—Ya empiezas a **tocarme los cojones** con tus problemas sexuales. Me importan una mierda. • You're beginning to piss me off with your sexual problems. I don't give a shit.

cojonudo/a *adj.*

SEXCELLENT, ACE

—*Me parece **cojonudo** que salgamos de excursión.* • *Sexcellent! Going on a trip? Yes!*

colar *v.*

1 TO (NOT) BUY IT

—*Vaya excusa te has inventado. No **cuela**, tío.* • *What an excuse you've made up. I'm not buying it.*

2 colado/a (estar) *loc.*

TO BE HUNG UP ON SOMETHING OR SOMEBODY

—*Está totalmente **colado** por esta chavala. Solo habla de ella.* • *He's totally hung up on that chick. He keeps going on and on about her.*

colega *n.*

MATE, DUDE

—*¡Qué pasa **colega**!* • *Wassup, dude!*

colgado/a *adj., n.*

1 GEEK, LOSER, FREAK

—*Miguel es un **colgado**. No hace nada en todo el día.* • *Miguel is a loser. He does nothing all day.*

2 dejar colgado/a *loc.*

TO LEAVE SOMEONE HIGH AND DRY

—*Me **dejaron colgado** en el garito ese.* • *They left me high and dry in that boozer.*

3 colgarse *v. prnl.*

TO FALL BEHIND

—*Esta semana **me he colgado** un poco. No sé si acabaré el trabajo para el jueves.* • *I've fallen behind a bit this week. I don't know if I'll finish the job by Thursday.*

colocón *n.*

TO BE OUT OF IT (ALCOHOL OR DRUGS)

—*¡Qué **colocón** llevo!* • *I'm out of it!*

columpiarse *v. prnl.*

1 TO FALL BEHIND

—*Me **he columpiado** mazo con este tema. A ver si me pongo las pilas.* • *I've really fallen behind with this subject. I'll need to get my finger out.*

2 TO BALLS SOMETHING UP

—*Este tío **se ha columpiado**. Todas las cifras están mal.* • *This guy's really ballsed it up. All the figures are wrong.*

LITERALLY COLUMPIARSE MEANS TO SWING. SO JUST IMAGINE ENJOYING YOURSELF ON A SWING INSTEAD OF WORKING

coña (de) *loc.*

1 JOKE, A PISS-TAKE

—*¿Estás de coña, no?* • *This is a piss-take, right?*

2 SUPERB

—*Comimos de coña en el restaurante del puerto. Estaba todo buenísimo.* • *We had a superb meal in the harbour restaurant. Everything was great.*

coñazo *n.*

A DEAD BORING THING

—*¡Qué coñazo tener que ir a casa de Pepe a comer!* • *It's dead boring going to Pepe's for lunch.*

correrse *v. prnl. (vul.)*

TO CUM

—*Las actrices porno simulan que se corren, no te creas que tienen orgasmos de verdad.* • *Porno actresses pretend to cum, don't believe they have real orgasms.*

cortado/a *adj.*

TO BE BACKWARDS AT COMING FORWARDS

—*Catalina es muy cortada.* • *Catalina is backwards at coming forwards.*

corte *n.*

TO BITE SOMEONE'S NOSE OFF

—*¡Qué corte me metió Gael el otro día!* • *Gael bit my nose off the other day.*

costo *n.*

HASH

—*¿Tienes costo, tío?* • *Got any hash, mate?*

crack *n.*

A SHARK

—*Mi hermano es un puto crack del billar.* • *My brother is an effing shark at pool.*

crudo (tenerlo) *loc.*

NOT GONNA HAPPEN

—*Lo de ir a esquiar este finde creo que lo tenemos crudo.* • *Ski-ing this weekend's not gonna happen.*

cuadros (quedarse a) *loc.*

TO BE GOBSMACKED

—*Me quedé a cuadros cuando me despidieron.* • *I was gobsmacked when they fired me.*

cuba (como una) *loc.*

PISSED [UK], WELLIED, WAZZED, HAMMERED, BLOTTO

—*Pablo estaba como una cuba*

en la fiesta. • *Pablo was blotto at the party.*

cubata *n.*
A SPIRIT AND A MIXER

—*María, ¿me pides un* **cubata**? • *Maria, can you get me a drink... erm... a spirit and a mixer... a G&T?*

cuchitril *n.*
A DUMP

—*Tu casa parece un* **cuchitril**. • *Your house looks like a dump.*

cuento chino *n.*
A WIND-UP, PORKIES

—*No me cuentes* **cuentos chinos**, *ya no creo nada de lo que dices.* • *Less of your porkies, I don't believe a thing you say.*

cuerno(s)
1 poner los cuernos *loc.*
TO CHEAT ON

—*Ahora ha sido ella la que le* **ha puesto los cuernos**. • *She's the one who's been cheating on him now.*

2 romperse los cuernos *loc.*
TO SLOG AWAY

—**Me rompo los cuernos** *un día sí y otro también y no recibo absolutamente nada a cambio. ¡No puedo más!* • *I slog away and get absolutely nowt in return. I can't take anymore.*

cuesco *n.*
AIR BISCUIT

—*¡Oh no! ¡Aquí huele a* **cuesco**! • *Oh no! I smell an air biscuit!*

culo
1 ASS, BUTT *n.*

—*Tiene un buen* **culo** *tu hermana.* • *Your sister's got a great ass.*

2 caer como el culo *loc.*
TO BE AN ASSHOLE

—*Si te digo la verdad, tu amigo* **me cae como el culo**. • *To tell you the truth, your mate's an asshole.*

3 quedar como el culo *loc.*
TO ACT LIKE AN ASSHOLE

—*Fernández* **quedó como el culo** *delante de todo el mundo. Llegó 10 minutos tarde a la reunión.* • *Fernández acted like an asshole in front of everybody. He arrived 10 minutes late for the meeting.*

4 partirse el culo *loc.*
TO SPLIT ONE'S ARSE LAUGHING

—*Mira este vídeo. Te vas a* **partir el culo**. • *Look at this video. You will split your arse laughing.*

5 mover el culo *loc.*
TO GET ONE'S FINGER OUT, TO MOVE YOUR ASS

—**Mueve el culo**, *tío, que te estás apalancando mogollón.* • *Get your finger out, mate! You are slobbing around.*

6 tonto/a del culo *loc.*

AN ASSHOLE, DAMN STUPID

—*Mi primo Javier es **tonto del culo**. Ahora dice que no me puede devolver la pasta que me debe.* • *My cousin Javier's an asshole. He says he can't pay back.*

7 culo y mierda *loc.*

HICCUP AND HEARTBURN

—*Obélix y Astérix son **culo y mierda**, siempre van juntos para partirles la cara a los romanos.* • *Obelix and Axterix are like hiccup and heartburn. They always go together to smash the Romans' faces in.*

currar *v.*

1 TO WORK

—*¿A qué hora sales de **currar**?* • *What time do you get off work?*

2 currárselo *v .prnl.*

TO GET ONE'S FINGER OUT

—*O **te lo curras** un poco, o Rosa va a seguir pasando de ti como de la mierda.* • *Get your finger out or Rosa won't pay you a blind bit of difference.*

3 currante *adj.*

HARD-WORKING

—*Julia es muy **currante**.* • *Julia's really hard-working.*

4 curro *n.*

WORK

—*María está hasta las narices del **curro**.* • *María is pissed off at work.*

cursi *adj.*

CHEESY, CORNY

—*Las historias románticas como la de "Titanic" son muy **cursis**, ¿no crees?* • *Romantic stories like "Titanic" are really cheesy. Don't you think?*

cutre *adj.*

TACKY

—*Eso que ha hecho tu hermana es muy **cutre**.* • *That's really tacky what your sister did.*

cutrerío, cutrez, cutrada *n.*

TACKINESS

—*Hacer las cosas así, sin ganas, rápido y mal es una **cutrez**.* • *This is total tackiness!*

¡TÍO, EN MENUDO EMBOLAO TE HAS METIDO! • OH MAN. YOU'RE REALLY IN THE SHIT, NOW

depre *adj.*
ON A DOWNER

—*Desde que Manolo la plantó, está muy **depre**.* • *Since Manolo chucked her, she's been on a real downer.*

descarado *adj.*
HELL YEAH, DO BEARS SHIT IN THE WOODS?

—*¿Sales está noche de farra con nosotros? //¡**Descarao!*** • *Are you hitting the town with us tonight? // Do bears shit in the woods?*

descojonarse *v. prnl.*
TO SPLIT ONE'S ARSE LAUGHING

—*¿Reírme? Me **descojoné**.* • *Laugh? I split my arse.*

desfasarse *v. prnl.*
TO GET SHIT-FACED

—*La verdad es que en la fiesta del viernes nos **desfasamos** un huevo.* • *Oh man, we got shit-faced on Friday night.*

desmadre *n.*
ALL HELL BROKE LOOSE

—*En la fiesta del viernes el **desmadre** fue tal que acabó viniendo la pasma.* • *All hell broke loose at the party on Friday, the pigs came.*

YOU CAN ALSO SAY
DESPIPORRE

despelotarse *v. prnl.*
TO GET ONE'S KIT OFF,
TO GO MAD

—*En la famosa fiesta la gente acabó **despelotándose**.* • *On that famous night out everybody ended up getting their kit off.*

despellejar *v.*
TO EAT SOMEONE ALIVE,
TO LAY INTO (CRITICISE)

—*Os estáis pasando, pobre chaval, lo estáis **despellejando** vivo.* • *You're out of order, poor kid, you're eating him alive.*

desplumar v.

TO GET ROBBED

—*Al pobre guiri lo* **desplumaron** *en aquel callejón.* • *That Johnny Foreigner got robbed down that little street.*

diálogo de besugos expr.

GOBBLEDYGOOK

—*El debate de ayer fue un* **diálogo de besugos.** *Cada uno a su bola sin escuchar al otro.* • *Yesterday's debate was pure gobbledygook. Everybody going on about their own thing and not listening to anybody.*

dólar (montarse en el) loc.

TO BE MINTED, FLUSH

—*José Javier está* **montado en el dólar,** *se ha vuelto a comprar otro BMW. ¡Ya tiene tres!* • *José Javier's minted, he's bought another BMW. That's his third!*

domingas n. pl.

BOOBS, MAMS, TITS, JUGS

—*No puedo evitar mirarle las* **domingas** *a la nueva chica de la oficina. Lo malo es que me ha pillado.* • *I can't help looking at the new girl's jugs. The bad thing is she caught me.*

dominguero/a n.

THIS IS THE PERSON WITH TOURISTY INTENTIONS WHO IS OUT FOR A DRIVE AT THE WEEKEND NORMALLY WITH ALL THE FAMILY SQUEEZED INTO A TINY CAR. THEY'RE NOT USUALLY VERY POPULAR AMONG OTHER NORMAL LOCALS

don nadie loc.

A LOSER, MR NOBODY

—*Mi vecino es un* **don nadie.** • *My neighbour's a loser.*

echao pa'lante *loc.*

A PERSON WITH "BALLS"

—*Mi novio es muy **echao pa'lante**, no le tiene miedo a nada.* • *My boyfriend's got balls, nothing scares him.*

embolado *n.*

A HEAVY SITUATION

—*¡Tío, en menudo **embolao** te has metido!* • *Oh, man. You've really got yourself into a heavy situation now.*

empalmarse *v. prnl. (vul.)*

TO GET A HARD ON,
TO GET A BONER

—*¡Nena cuando te acercas **me empalmo**!* • *Baby, when you come near me I get a hard on!*

YOU CAN ALSO SAY ESTAR PALOTE

empanarse *v. prnl.*

1 TO GET IT (UNDERSTAND)

—*Tío, no fumes tantos porros que luego no **te empanas** de nada.* • *Dude, don't smoke so many joints 'cos later you just won't get it.*

2 empanada *n.*

MENTAL DIARRHOEA

—*¡Vaya pedo anoche! Hoy llevo una **empanada** que te cagas.* • *What a bender last night! I've got total mental diarrhoea today.*

3 empanado/a *adj., n.*

A SPACE CADET, TO BE LIKE A FART IN A TRANCE

—*¡Estás **empanao**, tío, espabila!* • *You're like a fart in a trance, man. Wake up!*

empaparse *v. prnl.*

TO SUSS OUT

—*Antes de ir a Marruecos, pienso **empaparme** a fondo de su cultura.* • *Before going to Morocco, I'm gonna suss out their culture.*

empapelar *v.*

TO GET NICKED

—*A Richard le han **empapelado** por llevar 50 gramos de caballo.* • *Richard got nicked for carrying 50 grams of smack.*

empastillado/a _adj._
TO BE OUT OF IT (UNDER THE CHEMICAL INFLUENCE OF RECREATIONAL DRUGS)

—_Jaime siempre va_ **empastillado** _a las fiestas._ • _Jaime's always out of it at parties._

empollar _v._
SWOT FOR AN EXAM

—_Este finde me encierro para_ **empollar** _para el examen del martes._ • _I'm staying in this weekend to swot for Tuesday's exam._

emporrado/a _adj._
STONED

—_No me acuerdo de nada de la fiesta, me pasé la noche_ **emporrada**. • _I can't remember much about the party, I was stoned all night._

enchocharse _v. prnl._
TO BE HUNG UP ON A CHICK

—_¡Quién lo iba a decir de Alberto,_ **enchochado** _por una tía!_ • _Who would've thought that Alberto would be hung up on a chick?_

YOU CAN ENCOÑARTE AS WELL

enchufe _n._
NEPOTISM

—_La nueva chica ha entrado por_ **enchufe**, _es la sobrina del jefe._ •

The new girl got in by nepotism, she's the boss's niece.

enganchado/a _adj._
TO BE HOOKED ON SOMETHING

—_Mark está_ **enganchado** _al facebook._ • _Mark's hooked on facebook._

enrollarse _v. prnl._
1 TO GET OFF WITH, TO MAKE OUT

—_El fin de semana pasado_ **me enrollé** _con dos pavas: una el viernes y otra el sábado._ • _I got off with two birds at the weekend; one on Friday and another on Saturday._

2 TO GO ON AND ON

—_No_ **te enrolles** _tanto, pesao. ¡Ve al grano!_ • _Stop going on and on, you pain. Get to the point!_

3 enrollado/a _adj., n._
A COOL PERSON

—_Marco es un_ **enrollao**. • _Marco's cool._

entrar _v._
TO CHAT UP

—_Ayer en la fiesta_ **entré** _a tres pavas pero ninguna de las tres me hizo caso. Estoy acabao._ • _I chatted up these three birds last night and they all knocked me back. I'm finished._

SE HA FUNDIDO TODA
LA PASTA DE LA HERENCIA
DE SU MADRE EN DOS DÍAS.
HE BLEW ALL THE CHEDDA
FROM HIS MOM'S
INHERITANCE IN TWO DAYS

facha *n., adj.*
FASCIST

—*Este periódico es super**facha**.*
• *This paper is pure fascist.*

facu *n.*
(facultad)
UNI

—*Mañana no voy a la **facu** porque tengo que estudiar para el examen del viernes.* • *I'm not going into uni tomorrow. I've gotta swot up for Friday's exam.*

fardar *v.*
TO SHOW OFF, TO FLOSS

—*A mi padre le encanta **fardar** de nuevo coche.* • *My dad loves showing off when he's got a new car.*

farlopa *n.*
COKE, CHARLY, BLOW, SNIFF

—*Ese camello solo pasa **farlopa**.*
• *That dealer only does coke.*

farra *n.*
NIGHT OUT

—*¡Menuda **farra** el viernes! Todavía no me he recuperado.* • *What a night out on Friday! I'm still knackered.*

fashion *n., adj.*
IN, TRENDY

—*Este restaurante es muy **fashion** pero la comida es malísima.* • *This restaurant's really in, but the grub is crap.*

fibrado/a *adj.*
HUNK

—*¡Qué **fibrado** está tu novio! Está como un queso.* • *Your boyfriend's a pure hunk! He's really hot.*

fiesta (ir de) *loc.*
1 TO HIT THE TOWN

—*Esta noche nos vamos todos de **fiesta**.* • *We're gonna hit the town tonight.*

2 **fiestero/a** *n., adj.*
UP FOR THE PARTY

—*Carlos es el más **fiestero** de mis colegas.* • *Carlos is the one who's always up for the party.*

fijo *adv.*

UP FOR

—*Yo **fijo** que voy. Los demás, no tengo ni idea.* • *I'm up for going. The rest I dunno.*

finde *n.*

This is a short version of **fin de semana** (weekend). Sometimes to be cool in Spanish you can shorten the word, for example **facultad** (faculty) means "university". So, **facu** means "uni".

—*¿Al final qué hacemos este **finde**? ¿Nos vamos de excursión o qué? In the end, what are we doing this weekend? Are we going on a trip or what?*

flaseado/a *adj.*

FLOORED, SHOCKED

—*La noticia me ha dejado **flaseada**.* • *The news has left me floored.*

flash *n.*

SHOCK, FRIGHT

—*A mi madre le va a dar un buen **flash** cuando se entere.* • *My mum's gonna get a right shock when she finds out.*

flipar *v.*

1 TO BE GOBSMACKED

—*Me encanta este lugar, estoy **flipando**.* • *I love this place, I'm totally gobsmacked.*

2 TO BE PISSED OFF [UK], TO BE PISSED [USA]

—***Flipo** con María. Todavía no me ha felicitado por la boda.* • *I'm pissed off at María. She still hasn't congratulated me on the wedding.*

folla (tener mala) *loc.*

TO BE A BADASS MOFO, TO BE A MARDY COW (PARA CHICAS)

—*Ten cuidado con Albert que **tiene muy mala folla**.* • *Be careful with Albert. He's a badass mofo.*

follar *v. (vulg.)*

1 TO FUCK

—*Hace más de tres meses que no **follo**.* • *I haven't fucked for three months.*

2 follado/a *adj.*

TO GO LIKE THE CLAPPERS

—*Ese coche va **follao**. Seguro que va a más de ochenta por la ciudad.* • *This car goes like the clappers. It'll do more than 80 in the city.*

3 folleteo *n.*

SHAGGING

—*El **folleteo** y el fumeque es lo único que le interesa.* • *Shagging and skinning up are the only things that interest him.*

follón *n.*

MESS, CONFUSION

—*¡Qué **follón**!* • *What a mess!*

forrarse *v. prnl.*

1 TO GET MINTED

—*El tío se ha forrado con su página web. Y eso que al principio nadie daba un duro por él.* • *He got minted with his website. Before nobody rated him.*

2 forrado/a *adj.*

MINTED

—*Tim está forrado. Tiene más de 2 millones de euros en un banco suizo.* • *Tim's minted. He's got more than 2 million euros in a Swiss bank account.*

fregado *n.*

A HEAVY SITUATION

—*¡Vaya fregado! No sé cómo saldremos de ésta.* • *This is a heavy situation! I don't know how we're gonna get out of this.*

friqui *n.*

NERD

—*¡Eres un friqui! No me extraña que no ligues ni a la de tres.* • *You're a nerd! I'm not surprised you can't pull.*

frito/a *adj.*

KNACKERED, SHATTERED, FED UP

—*Estoy frito, tío. Esta noche no he dormido nada.* • *I'm shattered, man. I didn't sleep a wink last night.*

fuerte *adj.*

HEAVY

—*¡Qué fuerte lo de María! Eso sí que no me lo esperaba.* • *That's so heavy about María. I didn't see that coming.*

THE WORD HEAVY IS NOW COOL TO USE IN SPANISH. FOR EXAMPLE ¡QUÉ HEAVY!

fumeta *n.*

POTHEAD, STONER

—*El compañero de piso de Luis Fernández es un fumeta de mucho cuidado. No sé si le conviene mucho a Luis Fernández vivir con un pavo así.* • *Luis Fernández's flatmate is a total stoner. I don't think Luis Fernández should be mixing with a guy like this.*

fundirse *v. prnl.*

TO BLOW (MONEY)

—*Se ha fundido toda la pasta de la herencia de su madre en dos días.* • *He blew all the chedda from his mom's inheritance in two days.*

gafe *n., adj.*
A JINX

—*Andrés es un **gafe**, siempre que coge el ascensor se jode.* • *Andrés is a jinx. Every time he gets in the lift, it breaks down.*

gamba (meter la) *loc.*
TO BALLS SOMETHING UP,
TO FUCK SOMETHING UP

—***Has metido la gamba** hasta el fondo. A ver cómo lo arreglas ahora.* • *You've really fucked it up now. I'd like to see how you are gonna get out of that.*

ganga *n.*
BARGAIN

—*Mariluz solo compra **gangas** cuando va de compras.* • *Mariluz only buys bargains when she shops.*

ganso/a *adj.*
HUMUNGOUS

—*Vivimos en un piso super**ganso**.* • *We live in a humungous flat.*

garbeo (dar un) *loc.*
TO GO FOR A WANDER,
TO WANDER ABOUT

—*Me voy a **dar un garbeo**.* • *I'm going for a wander.*

YOU CAN ALSO DARTE UN RULO OR DARTE UN PIRULO

garito *n.*
BOOZER

—*Han abierto un **garito** muy guapo en el puerto.* • *They've opened a great little boozer down the harbour.*

garrafón *n.*
CHEAP BOOZE

—*¡Pedazo de resaca! Todo por culpa del **garrafón** que nos metieron anoche en el "Blues".* • *What a hangover! Thanks to all that cheap booze they were serving us in the "Blues".*

Garrafón actually refers to filling an empty bottle of quality booze with cheap shit. The kind of thing that really pisses the seasoned drinker off.

garrulo/a *n.*
LOUT

—*Este bar está lleno de **garrulos**. Nos piramos.* • *This boozer is full of louts. We're outta here.*

gasofa *n.*
PETROL, GAS

—*Tendremos que parar pronto porque nos estamos quedando sin **gasofa**.* • *We'll have to stop soon 'cos we're running out of gas.*

gatillazo *n.*
CAN'T GET IT UP

THIS IS THE STATE OF NOT BEING ABLE TO GET ONE'S PECKER UP

—*¡Qué vergüenza! Tres meses intentando llevarme al huerto a Raquel, y cuando finalmente lo consigo, ¡**gatillazo**!* • *What a red neck! I'd been trying for three months to get Raquel into the sack. When I finally did, I couldn't get it up!*

gayumbos *n. pl.*
SCANTS, UNDERPANTS

—*Súbete los pantalones porque se te ven mogollón los **gayumbos**.* • *Pull your trousers up, you can see your scants.*

gentuza *n.*
RIFF-RAFF, RABBLE

—*¡Qué **gentuza**!* • *What a rabble!*

gilipollas *n.*
DICKHEAD, KNOB, ASSHOLE

—*¡Qué **gilipollas** el tío! No ha querido participar en el regalo.* • *What an asshole! He didn't chip in for the present.*

gilipollez *n.*
1 CRAP, SHITE (NONSENSE)

—*Deberías cerrar el pico de vez en cuando, porque no dices más que **gilipolleces**.* • *You should shut your trap for a change, 'cos you talk nothing but shite.*

2 A BALLS UP, A FUCK UP

—*Dejar un trabajo así es una **gilipollez**.* • *You'll balls it all up leaving a job like that.*

golpe *n.*
1 A HOLD UP, A HIT (ROBBERY)

—*Han pillado a la banda de atracadores que daba **golpes** en bancos de pueblos.* • *They got the gang who were hitting the banks in the villages.*

2 golpe bajo *loc.*
BELOW THE BELT

—*Recordarle lo de su ex ha sido un **golpe bajo**.* • *Reminding her of her ex was a bit below the belt.*

3 no dar ni golpe *loc.*
TO DO FUCK ALL

—*El nuevo secretario no **da ni golpe**.* • *The new secretary does fuck all.*

goma *n.*

RUBBER, JOHNNY

—*¡Hay que joderse, no me queda ninguna **goma**!* • *Fuck's sake! I've run out of johnnies.*

gorila *n.*

BEAR

—*¡Vaya par de **gorilas** que hay en la puerta de ese garito!* • *There's right pair of bears on the door of that boozer.*

gorra (de) *loc.*

FOR FREE, FOR NOWT

—*He entrado **de gorra**.* • *I got in for nowt.*

gorronear *v.*

TO MOOCH, TO CADGE

—*¿Cuándo vas a comprar tabaco? Siempre estás **gorroneando** el mío.* • *When are you gonna buy some fags and stop mooching mine?*

guaperas *n.*

HUNK

—*¡Vaya **guaperas** el tío!* • *He's such a hunk!*

guarrada *n.*

A DIRTY TRICK, SOMETHING THAT'S NOT ON

—*Liarte con el novio de tu amiga es una **guarrada**.* • *Getting off with your mate's boyfriend is not on.*

guarro/a *adj., n.*

DIRTY PIG, MINGER

—*Es un **guarro**, siempre lleva gayumbos con frenazo.* • *He's a dirty pig, he's always wears pants with skid marks.*

guay *adj.*

COOL

—*¡Qué **guay** que vengas a mi fiesta!* • *That's cool that you're coming to my party!*

guiri *n.*

1 JOHNNY FOREIGNER

—*Los precios de Las Ramblas son para **guiris**.* • *You only get Johnny Foreigner prices down the Ramblas.*

2 guirilandia *n.*

TOURIST SPOTS, JOHNNY FOREIGNER LAND

—*Me encanta salir por **guirilandia**, está lleno de tíos buenos.* • *I love going out in tourist spots, it's full of hunks.*

gusanillo *n.*

The "munchies" when it comes to hunger and a "craving" or "itching" for anything else.

—*De tanto hablar de comida me ha entrado el **gusanillo**.* • *All this talking about food has given me the munchies.*

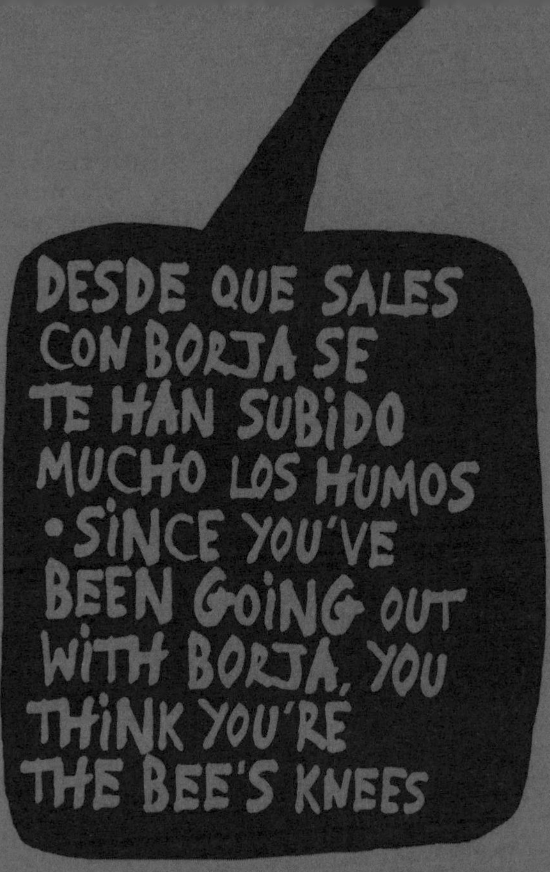
DESDE QUE SALES CON BORJA SE TE HAN SUBIDO MUCHO LOS HUMOS • SINCE YOU'VE BEEN GOING OUT WITH BORJA, YOU THINK YOU'RE THE BEE'S KNEES

hervor (faltar un) *loc.*
TO BE WET BEHIND THE EARS

—*Este chico es muy inmaduro, todavía le falta un hervor.* • *This guy's a bit wet behind the ears.*

hierba *n.*
GRASS, WEED

—*Lo entrullaron por vender hierba en la puerta del insti.* • *He got nicked for dealing grass at the school gates.*

hijoputa *n.*
WANKER, MOFO

—*¡Qué hijoputa!* • *What a wanker!*

hortera *adj.*
1 NAFF, TACKY

—*Sonia es muy hortera.* • *Sonia's really tacky.*

2 horterada *n.*
SOMETHING THAT'S REALLY NAFF

—*Tío, regalarle a tu novia flores el día de San Valentín es una horterada.* • *Oh, Man! Getting your bird flowers on Valentine's day is really naff.*

hostia *n.*
This is one of those multi-purpose words which you really need to be cool in Spanish. **Hostia** literally means "the host" (communion) which is the reason for the word's naughtiness. Let's have a look at its usefulness as well as its naughtiness.

—*¡Hostia!* • *Bloody hell!*

—*¡Esto es la hostia!* • *This is fucking brilliant!*

—*¡Te voy a dar un par de hostias!* • *I'm gonna deck you!*

—*¿Qué hostias haces aquí?* • *What the fuck are you doing here?*

hostiar *v.*
1 TO DECK

—*Te voy a hostiar como sigas mirándome así.* • *I'm gonna deck you if you keep looking at me like that.*

2 hostión *n.*

A BANG (A HIT)

—*Se ha dado un buen **hostión** con el coche.* • *He gave the car a right bang.*

huevo

1 un huevo *adv.*

SO, PURE

—*Me gusta **un huevo** tu nueva chupa.* • *I so like your new jacket.*

2 un huevo de *adv.*

A HUMUNGOUS AMOUNT

—*Mi primo tiene **un huevo de** motos; seis o siete, creo.* • *My cousin's got a humungous amount of bikes; six or seven I think.*

3 tener huevos *loc.*

TO HAVE BALLS, TO HAVE BOLLOCKS, TO HAVE NUTS

—*No tuvo **huevos** para hacerlo* • *He didn´t have the balls to do it*

4 tocarse los huevos *loc.*

TO SCRATCH ONE'S BALLS

—*Albert no ha avanzado en el dosier. Se ha estado **tocando los huevos** toda la mañana.* • *Albert hasn't progressed with the dossier. He's been scratching his balls all morning.*

SCRATCH IS RASCARSE IN SPANISH AND YOU CAN ALSO USE THIS VERB. SO FEEL FREE TO SCRATCH YOUR BALLS IN SPANISH TOO

humo

1 bajar los humos *loc.*

TO HAVE SOMEONE UNDER THE THUMB, TO PUT SOMEONE UNDER THE THUMB

—*Lo que tú necesitas es que alguien te **baje los humos**.* • *What you need is for somebody to put you under the thumb.*

2 subírsele los humos *loc.*

TO THINK YOU'RE THE BEE'S KNEES

—*Desde que sales con Borja se te han **subido** mucho **los humos**.* • *Since you've been going out with Borja, you think you're the bee's knees.*

ANOTHER EXPRESSION IS CREERSE EL REY O LA REINA DEL MAMBO. WHICH DO YOU PREFER?

3 vender humo *loc.*

TO TALK SHITE, TO TALK BOLLOCKS, TO BE ALL SMOKE AND MIRRORS

—*No te creas ni media palabra de ese tío. Solo **vende humo**.* • *Don't believe a word the guy says. He's talking shite.*

iluminado/a *n.*

THE SPECIAL ONE

—*Este tío se cree que tiene poderes especiales. Es un **iluminado**.* • *This guy thinks he's got special powers. He's the special one.*

insti *n.*

The diminutive for "high school". A common way of speaking informally in Spanish is to shorten words.

—*¿A qué hora sales del **insti**?* • *What time do you finish school?*

intelectualoide *n.*

A PSEUDO-INTELLECTUAL

—*Este café está lleno de **intelectualoides**.* • *This cafe's full of pseudo-intellectuals.*

invento (joderse el) *loc.*

TO BALLS SOMETHING UP

—*¡Vaya mierda, ya **se jodió el invento**!* • *You've really ballsed it up now.*

J

jalar *v.*
TO TUCK AWAY, TO POLISH OFF

—*En la fiesta de Juan no había nada para **jalar**.* • *We didn't have much to tuck away at Juan's party.*

jamona *adj. y n.*
WOMAN WITH CHILD-BEARING HIPS, BOOTYLICIOUS

—*A mí me molan las tías **jamonas**.* • *I love bootylicious women.*

jeta (tener) *loc.*
TO BE WIDE, TO BE DODGY

—*Ten cuidado que tiene mucha **jeta**.* • *Be careful, he's really wide.*

jiñarse *v. prnl.*
TO BRICK IT, TO SHIT IT

—*Cada vez que vuela **se jiña**.* • *Every time he flies he bricks it.*

jipiar *v.*
TO SEE

—*Me voy unas filas más adelante; aquí no **jipio** nada.* • *I'm going a couple of rows up. I can't see anything from here.*

joder *v.*
1 TO FUCK UP

—*Me estás **jodiendo** la vida.* • *You're fucking my life up.*

2 joderse *v. prnl.*
TO BREAK DOWN, TO BE FUCKED

—*No podemos ir porque **se me ha jodido** el coche.* • *We can't go 'cos the car's fucked.*

3 joderla *loc.*
TO BALLS UP, TO FUCK UP

—*La has vuelto a **joder**.* • *You've fucked up again.*

4 ¡joder! *interj.*
The most popular exclamation between Spaniards to show anger, astonishment, amazement, happiness, or absolutely anything. Euphemisms and substitutes are: ¡Jo!, ¡Jobar!, ¡Jolín!, ¡Jolines!, etc.

jodido/a *adj., adv.*
FUCKING, FUCKED, FUCKED UP

—*¡Eres un **jodido** cabrón!* • *You are a fucking wanker!*

—*La situación está **jodida**.* • *It's all fucked up.*

—*Desde el accidente tengo la pierna **jodida**.* • *My leg's been fucked since the accident.*

ÉRAMOS CIENTO Y LA MADRE EN LA FIESTA • EVERYBODY AND THEIR DOG WAS AT THE PARTY
TUVIMOS MOVIDA CON LOS VECINOS POR LO DE LA FIESTA • WE HAD A RIGHT DING DONG WITH THE NEIGHBOURS ABOUT THE PARTY

labia *n.*

LIPPY, MOUTHY

—*Mejor que hables tú, que tienes mucha **labia**.* • *You'd better do the talking, you're the mouthy one.*

lameculos *n.*

ARSELICKER

—*Le ascendieron porque es un **lameculos**, no por otra cosa.* • *He only got the promotion because he's an arselicker.*

lapa *n.*

LEECH

—*Eres una **lapa**, estás todo el día pegado a mi. Déjame respirar.* • *You spend all day stuck to me like a leech. Give me breathing space.*

lapo *n.*

GROG

—*¡Qué asco, me acaban de tirar un **lapo**!* • *Shit! Somebody's just grogged on me!*

largar *v.*

1 TO TELL EVERYBODY, TO GOSSIP

—*No le cuentes nada a Pedro que lo **larga** todo.* • *Don't tell Pedro, he'll tell everybody.*

2 largarse *v. prnl.*
TO SHOOT OFF

—*¡Qué rollo, yo **me largo**!* • *This is crap, I'm gonna shoot off!*

largas (dar) *loc.*

TO SPIN SOME STORY

—*He intentado quedar con él, pero siempre **me da largas**.* • *I've tried to meet up with him, but he always spins some story.*

lata *n.*

A BUMMER

—*Es una **lata** trabajar los domingos.* • *Working on Sundays is a bummer.*

leche *n.*

1 CRACK, BANG, WALLOP

—*¡Vaya **leche** que se ha metido en las escaleras! ¡Pobrecito!* • *He's given himself a right crack on those stairs! Poor kid!*

2 la leche *expr.*
THE BUSINESS, SEXCELLENT
—*¡Esta peli es la **leche**!* • *The movie is the business!*

lefa *n. (vul.)*
SPUNK

legal *adj.*
SOUND (TRUSTWORTHY)
—*No te preocupes. Es un tío **legal**.* • *Don't worry. He's sound.*

leñazo *n.*
CRACK, BANG, WALLOP
—*Pues yo me acabo de dar un buen **leñazo** con la puerta del armario.* • *I've just given myself a right bang with the cupboard door.*

leonera *n.*
PIGSTY, A REAL STATE
—*Necesito ordenar mi habitación porque parece una auténtica **leonera**.* • *I'll need to tidy up my room, it's a real state.*

liado/a *adj.*
1 TO BE UP TO HERE WITH WORK OR STUFF
—*No puedo quedar esta tarde, estoy muy **liado**.* • *I can't meet up this afternoon, I'm up to here with stuff.*

2 TO BE AN ITEM
—*Mark y Almu están **liados**.*
• *Mark and Almu are an item.*

liar *v.*
1 TO ROLL OR TO SKIN UP (A CIGARETTE OR A JOINT)
—*Soy malísimo **liando**.* • *I'm shit at rolling.*

2 liarla *loc.*
TO GO MENTAL
—*¡Cómo **la liaste** ayer en la reunión!* • *You really went mental in the meeting yesterday.*

3 liarse *v. prnl.*
TO GET OFF WITH, TO MAKE OUT
—*Raúl **se lió** con una alumna.* • *Raúl got off with a student.*

TO BE ALL OVER THE PLACE
—***Me estoy liando** con tanto número.* • *I'm all over the place with these figures.*

ligar *v.*
1 TO PULL, TO GET OFF WITH SOMEONE
—*En este garito no se **liga** nada, yo me largo.* • *You can't pull in this boozer. I'm out of here.*

2 ligón *n.*
DON JUAN
—*Mi hermano es un **ligón**.* • *My brother is a Don Juan.*

3 ligoteo *n.*

THE ACT OF BEING ON
THE PULL

—*¡Hay que ver cómo te gusta el* **ligoteo**! • *You love being on the pull, don't ya?*

limpio/a *adj.*

CLEAN

—*Buscaron la ficha del sospechoso y estaba completamente* **limpio**. • *They looked at the suspect's record and he was completely clean.*

liquidar *v.*

1 TO DOWN (LIQUID)

—*¿Cuántos cubatas te has* **liquidado** *ya?* • *How many shots have you downed?*

2 TO HIT, WHACK (KILL)

—*Han* **liquidado** *a un capo de la Mafia.* • *They've whacked the Mafia boss.*

listillo/a *n.*

A KNOW-IT-ALL

—*¡Menuda* **listilla** *que estás hecha!* • *What a little know-it-all!*

litrona *n.*

A litre bottle of beer, which in English speaking culture would be a keg. These are popular for the **botellón** (the big booze-up with carryouts) which was a norm in the town squares near the bar zones of any Spanish town till the local government cracked down on it and sent it underground.

—*Vamos a comprar unas* **litronas** *para el botellón.* • *We're gonna buy a couple of kegs for the booze-up.*

loba *n.*

A SLUT, A TART, A SLAPPER

—*¡Vaya* **loba** *la tía esa! Le ha robado el novio a la Mari.* • *What a slut! She waltzed off with Mari's boyfriend.*

longuis (hacerse el) *loc.*

TO PLAY THE FOOL

—*No* **te hagas el longuis** *y suelta la pasta.* • *Stop playing the fool and splash the cash.*

loro (al) *loc.*

TO HAVE IT SUSSED,
TO WATCH OUT

—*Tienes que estar más* **al loro** *tío, que te las cuelan todas.* • *You have to have it sussed, they'll just take the piss.*

lote (darse el) *loc.*

TO SUCK FACE, TO TONGUE

—*Susana estaba* **dándose el lote** *en la puerta del baño.* • *Susana was sucking face at the toilet doors.*

macarra _n._
A HOOLIGAN

—_Desde que sale con esos, se ha vuelto un poco **macarra**._ • _Since he's been hanging up with them, he's turned into a hooligan._

machacar _v._
1 TO HUMP, TO THRASH

—_No solo perdimos, nos **machacaron**._ • _We didn't just lose, they humped us._

2 machacársela _v. prnl. (vul.)_
TO WANK

macizo/a _adj., n._
HOT, A RIDE, A BABE

—_¡La novia de Mark está **macizorra**!_ • _Mark's bird's hot!_

madero _n._
PIG, BACON

—_Más vale que paremos la fiesta, hay un par de **maderos** en la calle._ • _We should stop the party, there's couple of pigs outside._

madre
1 de puta madre _loc._
ACE, FUCKING BRILLIANT

—_¡Es **de puta madre** que trabajes con nosotros!_ • _That's fucking brilliant that you're working with us!_

2 ¡tu puta madre! _expr._
FUCK YOU!

3 ciento y la madre _loc._
EVERYBODY AND THEIR DOG

—_Éramos **ciento y la madre** en la fiesta._ • _Everybody and their dog was at the party._

majara _adj._
MENTAL, BONKERS, NUTS

—_Como siga trabajando a ese ritmo se va a volver **majara**._ • _If he keeps working like this, he'll go mental._

mamada _n. (vul.)_
A BLOWJOB

—_Nunca he hecho una **mamada** y nunca lo voy a hacer._ • _I've never given a blowjob and I'll never do it._

mamado/a _adj._

PISSED [UK], BLOTTO, WAZZED, BLIND, BLITZED

—*No solo Antonio, todo el mundo iba súper **mamado**.* • *It wasn't just Antonio, everybody was wazzed.*

mamón/a _n._

PRICK, DORK, DIPSTICK, DICKHEAD, TWAT

—*¡Eres un **mamón**! Deja de rajar de todo quisqui.* • *You're such a prick! Stop slagging everybody off.*

manazas _n., adj._

KLUTZ

—*No toques eso, que eres un **manazas**.* • *Don't touch that, you klutz.*

mandanga _n._

CRAP (TALK)

—*Déjate de **mandangas** y ve al grano.* • *Stop talking crap and get to the point.*

mangar _v._

TO GANK, TO NICK

—*¿Me has **mangado** el boli? Pero qué morro tienes.* • *Did you gank my pen? You've got no shame.*

mani, manifa _n._

DEMO (DEMONSTRATION)

—*¿Vienes a la **mani** del sábado?* •

Are you going on the demo on Saturday?

manitas _n._

1 A HANDYMAN

—*Tom es un **manitas**, sabe hacer de todo.* • *Tom's a handyman, he can do anything.*

2 hacer manitas _loc._

TO HOLD HANDS

—*Esos dos se pasan toda la clase **haciendo manitas** por debajo de la mesa.* • *Those two spend the whole class holding hands under the table.*

mantero _n._

HAWK

—*Lo conseguirás más barato de los **manteros** de la Gran Vía.* • *You'll get cheaper from the hawks on the Gran Vía.*

maquearse _v. prnl._

1 TO BE OR TO GET FITTED, TO BE OR TO GET KITTED OUT

—*¿Para quién **te has maqueado** tanto?* • *Who did you get kitted out for?*

2 maqueado/a _adj._

FITTED, KITTED OUT

—*¿Dónde vas tan **maqueado**? ¿A una boda?* • *Where are you going so kitted out? A wedding?*

marcha (ir de) *loc.*

TO HIT THE TOWN

—*No hagas planes para esta noche,* **nos vamos de marcha** *con la peña.* • *Don't make plans for tonight, we're hitting the town with the guys.*

maría *n.*

MARIJUANA, GRASS, WEED

—*¿Conoces a alguien que pase* **maría** *por aquí?* • *Know anybody who deals grass around here?*

mariconada *n. (vul.)*

BULLSHIT, CRAP

—*Lo que has hecho ha sido una* **mariconada**. • *What you've done is just bullshit.*

marimacho *n., adj.*

GEEZER BIRD

—*La hija de Pepe es un poco* **marimacho**. *Pero juega muy bien al fútbol.* • *Pepe's daughter's a bit of a geezer bird. But she's good at football.*

maromo *n.*

BLOKE, GUY

—*El* **maromo** *de tu hermana va en un coche tuneado, ¿no?* • *Your sister's bloke's got a souped up car, ain't he?*

marrón *n.*

A STICKY SITUATION

—*En menudo* **marrón** *te ha metido tu colega.* • *Your mate's got you in a right sticky situation now.*

marujear *v.*

1 TO GOSSIP

—*Basta de* **marujear** *y vuelve al curro.* • *Stop gossiping and get back to work.*

2 maruja *n.*

A SWEETY WIFE, A GOSSIP

—*¿Quién ha dicho que marujear es solo de chicas? Mira a Marcos, es* **supermaruja**. • *Who said gossiping was for women? Take Marcos, he's a total sweety wife.*

más (lo) *loc.*

THE BUSINESS

—*Este diccionario es* **lo más**. • *This dictionary is the business.*

masoca *n.*

MASOCHIST

—*Soy un* **masoca**, *esa tía no hace más que darme largas y yo ahí dale que te pego.* • *I'm a masochist. That bird's always knocking me back and I keep going after her.*

matasanos *n.*

A QUACK

—*Voy a cambiarme de médico porque el que tengo es un* **matasanos**. • *I'm gonna change doctors, this guy's a quack.*

mazo *adv.*

A STONKING OR HUMUNGOUS
AMOUNT

It's often used followed by the
preposition **de** plus noun.

—*Había **mazo** de gente en la fiesta.*
• *The party was full of deadbeats.*

michelines *n. pl.*

LOVE HANDLES

—*¡Nena cómo me ponen tus **michelines**!* • *Baby, your love handles
turn me on!*

mierda *n.*

1 AN ASSHOLE, A DICKHEAD

—*Deja a ese tío de una vez , no ves
que es un **mierda**.* • *Leave this guy,
can't you see he's an asshole?*

2 ON A BENDER (ALCOHOL
RELATED)

—*¡Vaya **mierda** que llevo!* • *I'm on
a bender!*

3 una mierda

SHITE, CRAP

—*Este CD es **una mierda**. Pon
otra cosa.* • *This CD's shite. Put
something else on.*

4 importar una mierda *loc.*

TO NOT GIVE A SHIT

—**Me importa una mierda** *si me
llama o no me llama. Paso totalmente del tema.* • *I don't give a shit if he
calls or not. I'm so over it.*

mogollón *adv.*

HUMUNGOUS, LOADS

It's often used followed by the
preposition **de** plus noun.

—*Había **mogollón** de peña en la
fiesta.* • *There was a humungous
amount of people at the party.*

mojar *v.*

1 TO GET SOME ACTION,
TO PULL

—*¿**Mojaste** ayer o qué? // Qué va,
tío, últimamente estoy a dos velas.*
• *Did you get any action last night
or what? // No way man, I just can't
pull lately.*

2 mojarse *v. prnl.*

TO CALL IT

—*Va, **mójate**. ¿Quién ganará la
Champions?* • *Come on , call it!
Who's gonna win the Champions'
League?*

molar *v.*

TO DIG, TO FEEL, TO ROCK

—*¡Tío me **mola** mogollón tu carro!*
• *Man, I really dig your car.*

mono/a *adj.*

1 CUTE

—*Es muy **mono** el novio de Sonia.
Y muy simpático.* • *Sonia's guy's so
cute! And really nice too.*

2 tener mono de *loc.*

TO HAVE A CRAVING FOR

—*Tengo mono de chocolate.* • *I've got a craving for chocolate.*

montón (un) *adv.*
A HUMUNGOUS AMOUNT

—*Tengo un montón de dinero.* • *I've got a humungous amount of cash.*

moño (estar hasta el) *loc.*
TO BE FED UP

—*Estoy hasta el moño de que no me acompañes nunca a hacer la compra.* • *I'm fed up with you never coming shopping.*

morbo (dar) *loc.*
THE STATE OF BEING TURNED ON

—*A mí ese tío me da morbo.* • *That guy turns me on.*

morrearse *v. prnl.*
1 TO SUCK FACE, TO TONGUE SOMEONE

—*Se estaban morreando en la puerta del baño.* • *They were sucking face at the toilet door.*

2 morreo *n.*
A SNOG

—*Solo se dieron un morreo. Eso sí, de más de dos minutos.* • *They just gave each other a snog. But a two-minute one.*

morro
1 tener morro *loc.*
TO BE WIDE

—*Tu jefe tiene mucho morro. Siempre se está aprovechando de ti.* • *Your boss is really wide. He's always taking advantage of you.*

2 echarle morro *loc.*
TO DARE

—*Ayer verdaderamente le echaste mucho morro cuando le dijiste al jefe lo que pensabas.* • *That was really daring of you to tell the boss what you thought yesterday.*

3 poner morros *loc.*
TO GET PISSED OFF,
TO GET HACKED OFF

—*Poniendo morros no conseguirás nada.* • *Getting pissed off about it will get you nowhere.*

4 por el morro *loc.*
FOR NOWT

—*Conseguimos entrar en ese garito por el morro.* • *We got into that place for nowt.*

USING ENGLISH WORDS IS COOL IN SPANISH BUT THEY'RE NOT ALWAYS UNDERSTOOD BY AN ENGLISH SPEAKER.

FOR EXAMPLE YOU CAN SUBSTITUTE POR EL MORRO WITH BY THE FACE

mosca (estar) *loc.*

TO BE PISSED OFF

—*Mi novia **está mosca** porque no le ha caído nada por San Valentín. A ver cómo lo soluciono.* • *My girlfriend is pissed off because she didn't get anything for Valentine's day. I'll see what I can do about it.*

moscas (por si las) *loc.*

JUST IN CASE

—*Mejor salir con tiempo, **por si las moscas**.* • *Better leave on time, just in case.*

YOU CAN ALSO SAY POR SI ACASO OR IF YOU WANT TO BE REALLY COOL POR SI ACA

mosquearse *v. prnl.*

1 TO GET HACKED OFF, TO GET PISSED OFF

—*Mi hermana **se ha mosqueado** conmigo, pero no sé por qué.* • *My sister's pissed off at me but I don't know why.*

2 mosqueo *n.*

A FOUL MOOD

—*Se fue a la cama con un buen **mosqueo**. A ver cómo se levanta mañana.* • *She went to bed in a foul mood. I don't know what she'll be like tomorrow.*

moto (vender la) *loc.*

TO TALK SHITE

—***No me vendas la moto**. Tú no conoces a Fernando Torres.* • *Don't talk shite. You've never met Fernando Torres.*

movida *n.*

A DING DONG, ARGY BARGY

—*Tuvimos **movida** con los vecinos por lo de la fiesta.* • *We had a right ding dong with the neighbours about the party.*

muermo *n.*

A SQUARE

—*Por favor no invites a Federico a la fiesta, que es un **muermo**.* • *Please don't invite Federico to the party, he's a square.*

muerte

1 de muerte *loc.*

SUPERB

—*¡Esta paella está **de muerte**!* • *This paella's superb!*

2 de mala muerte *loc.*

BADASS

—*Me han dicho que el concierto es en un garito **de mala muerte**.* • *I heard the gig's at a badass dump of a pub.*

nabo *n.*

COCK, DICK, KNOB, WILLIE,
TODGER, SAUSAGE, ONE-EYED
TROUSER SNAKE

IN SPANISH NABO IS TURNIP.
INTERESTING THAT,
ISN'T IT? DIFFERENT
CULTURES, DIFFERENT IDEAS

narices

1 estar hasta las narices *loc.*

TO BE FED UP

—***Estoy hasta las narices*** de este curro. • *I'm fed up with this job.*

2 meter las narices *loc.*

TO STICK ONE'S NOSE IN

—*A la vecina le encanta **meter las narices** donde no debe.* • *The neighbour loves sticking her nose in where it doesn't belong.*

4 por narices *loc. adv.*

BY BRUTE FORCE

—*Abrirá la puerta **por narices**.* • *He'll open the door by brute force.*

negado/a *adj., n.*

TO BE CRAP AT

—*Soy **negada** para los idiomas.* • *I'm crap at languages.*

nenaza *adj., n.*

A BIG CHICKEN, A WEED,
A WOOSE, A WUSS

—*Fran es una **nenaza**, llora hasta por una simple inyección.* • *Fran's a big chicken, crying over a jab.*

niñato/a *n.*

PRETENTIOUS GIT

—*Raúl es un **niñato**.* • *Raúl's a pretentious git.*

notas *n.*

A SHOW OFF

—*Entre las gafas de sol, la chupa y el coche tuneao, he flipao con tu colega. ¡Es un **notas**!* • *With the shades, the jacket and the souped-up car, I can't believe your mate. He's a show off!*

numerito *n.*

A HISSY FIT

—*Ha montado un **numerito** por una chorrada.* • *He had a hissy fit over nothing.*

okupa *n.*
SQUATTER

—*¿Te vienes a la fiesta en la casa* **okupa**? • *Are you going to the squatters' party?*

ojo *n.*
WATCH OUT

—**Ojo** *con el escalón, no te vayas a caer.* • *Watch out with the step, you're gonna fall.*

olla *n.*
1 NUT, NOGGIN

—*Tú estás mal de la* **olla**, *tío.* • *You're nuts, mate.*

2 írsele la olla *loc.*
TO LOSE IT

—*¡Cálmate, tío! Que* **se te va la olla**. • *Take it easy, mate! You're losing it!*

ordenata *n.*
COMPUTER, PC

—*¡Qué putada! Se me ha jodido el* **ordenata**. • *What a bummer! My PC's fucked!*

ostra
1 aburrirse como una ostra *loc.*
TO GET AS BORED AS FUCK

—**Me aburrí como una ostra** *en la fiesta.* • *I was as bored as fuck at the party.*

2 ¡ostras! *interj.*
BLOODY HELL

—**¡Ostras**, *tío, cuánto tiempo sin verte! ¿Dónde has estado?* • *Bloody hell, mate! I haven't seen you for ages! Where have you been?*

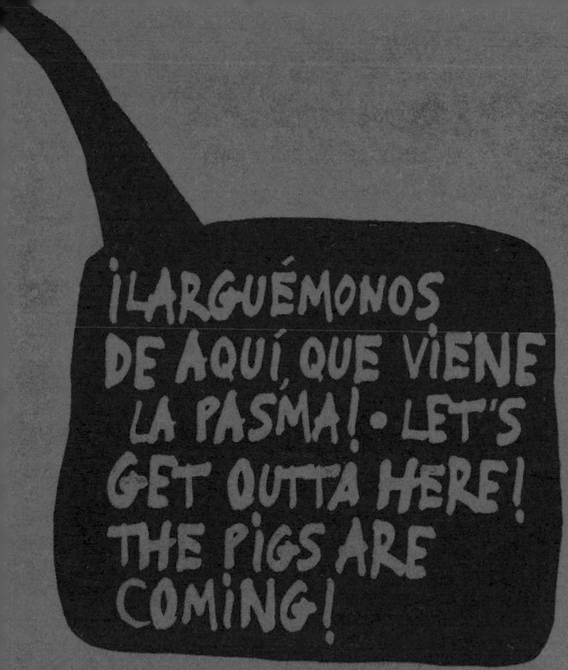
¡LARGUÉMONOS DE AQUÍ QUE VIENE LA PASMA! • LET'S GET OUTTA HERE! THE PIGS ARE COMING!

pachanguero/a _adj._
CHEESY

—_¡Oye, hortera! Deja de poner música tan **pachanguera**, por favor._ • _Hey, cheese ball! Stop putting the cheesy music on that record player, please._

pachas (pagar a) _loc._
TO SPLIT IT, TO GO DUTCH

—_Pagamos a **pachas**, ¿vale? Que no tengo mucha pasta._ • _We'll split it, OK? I don't have much dough._

YOU CAN SAY PAGAR A ESCOTE TOO

pachorra _n._
TO BE LAID BACK

—_Mark, ¡qué **pachorra** la tuya!, ¿no tendrías que estar en el curro ya?_ • _Mark, you're so laid back. Shouldn't you be at work?_

paganini _n._
THE SUCKER WHO ALWAYS PAYS

—_¡Estoy hasta los huevos de ser siempre el **paganini** del grupo!_ • _I'm up to here with being the sucker who always pays!_

paja _n._
1 A WANK

—_¡Qué cerdo, se estaba haciendo una **paja** en el baño!_ • _What a pig! He was having a wank in the toilets!_

2 paja mental _loc._
A HAMSTERWHEEL BRAIN

—_¿Por qué te haces tantas **pajas mentales**?_ • _Why do you always have a hamsterwheel brain?_

paleto/a _n._
LOUT

—_No tienes ni idea, eres un **paleto**._ • _You haven't got a clue, you lout._

paliza
1 dar la paliza _loc._
TO GO ON AND ON, TO BUG

—_No me **des la paliza** que me duele la cabeza._ • _Stop going on and on, I've got a headache._

2 dar una paliza _loc._
TO DECK, TO BEAT UP, TO HUMP (IN A GAME), THRASH

—**Nos dieron una paliza** _en la final de Copa._ • _We got humped in the Cup final._

palmar *v.*

1 TO POP ONE'S CLOGS,
TO KICK THE BUCKET

—*Su abuela la **palmó** la semana
pasada. Tenía 87 años.* • *Her granny kicked the bucket last week. She
was 87 years old.*

2 TO THROW IT AWAY,
TO LOSE

—*Entrenador: Como sigamos
jugando de esta manera en la segunda parte, vamos a **palmar** seguro.*
• *Coach: If we keep playing like this
in the second half, we're gonna throw
it away.*

palo *n.*

1 A BLOW, A SHOCK

—*La muerte de su madre fue un
palo para él.* • *His mum's death
was a blow to him.*

2 A DRAG

—*¡Qué **palo** me da la cena de esta
noche! No me apetece nada.* • *What
a drag having this dinner tonight. I
can't be bothered.*

pandero *n.*

BOOTY, BOOTIE

—*¡Guau! ¡Eso es un buen **pandero**, y lo demás son tonterías!* • *Hot!
That truly is a great booty and the
rest don't do anything for me!*

papa (ni) *loc.*

TO NOT HAVE A CLUE

—*No entiendo **ni papa** de lo que me
estás diciendo.* • *I don't have a clue
what you're talking about.*

IN TIMES OF TROUBLE
YOU CAN ALSO SAY
NI JOTA

papear *v.*

1 TO MUNCH

—*¿Hay algo para **papear** en la
nevera?* • *Is there anything to munch
in the fridge?*

2 papeo *n.*

GRUB

—*¿Habrá **papeo** en la fiesta?*
• *Will there be grub at the party?*

papeleo *n.*

PAPERWORK

—*Mañana tenemos que hacer todo
el **papeleo** de la compra de la nueva
casa.* • *We've got to do all the paperwork for the new house tomorrow.*

paquete *n.*

PACKET, WANGER

—*Me han dicho que tiene un buen
paquete; vamos, que está bien dota-
do.* • *I've heard he's got a large packet, you know, he's got a big wanger.*

pardillo/a *n., adj.*

SAP

—*El pobre Luis es muy **pardillo**, todo el mundo le vacila.* • *Poor Luis. He's a total sap, everybody takes the piss out of him.*

parida *n.*

JIBBER-JABBER

—*¡No dices más que **paridas**, cállate un poquito!* • *Less of your jibber-jabber, just shut it!*

parienta (la) *n.*

HER INDOORS

—*Esta noche voy al cine con **la parienta**.* • *I'm going to the flicks with her indoors tonight.*

parra (en la) *loc.*

TO BE A SPACE CADET, TO HAVE YOUR HEAD IN THE CLOUDS

—*Está **en la parra**. No sabía que George Bush ya no era el presidente de los Estados Unidos.* • *He's a space cadet, he didn't know that George Bush wasn't the president anymore.*

partes (las) *n. pl.*

ONE'S RUDE BITS, SEXUAL ORGANS

—*Le dieron una patada en **las partes**.* • *He got a kick in his rude bits.*

partirse *v. prnl.*

1 TO SPLIT ONE'S ARSE LAUGHING

—*¡Eres la leche, tía, contigo **me parto**!* • *You're a funny girl, with you I always end up splitting my arse laughing.*

2 partir la cara a alguien *loc.*

TO DECK SOMEONE

—*Un día de estos le voy a **partir la cara**, ya verás.* • *One of these days I'm gonna deck him, you'll see.*

pasada (una) *adj.*

ACE, SEXCELLENT

—*Las playas de esta costa son **una pasada**.* • *The beaches on this coast are ace.*

pasado/a *adj.*

1 STONED, A BIT OUT OF

—*Jorge iba muy **pasado** en la fiesta del viernes.* • *Jorge was a bit out of it at Friday's party.*

2 SO YESTERDAY

—*¡Quítate esa chupa! ¡Está **pasadísima**!* • *Get rid of the jacket! It's so yesterday!*

pasar *v.*

1 TO NOT BE INTO SOMETHING, TO GIVE SOMEONE A DEAF EAR

—*Yo **paso** de salir esta noche.* • *I'm not into going out tonight.*

—*¿Estás **pasando** de mí?* • *Are you giving me a deaf ear?*

2 TO DEAL DRUGS

—*Este camello **pasa** coca por la Plaza Real.* • *That D-boy deals coke in Plaza Real.*

3 ¿qué pasa? *expr.*

WHAT'S UP!, WASSUP!

4 pasarse tres pueblos *loc.*

TO BE OUT OF ORDER

—*¡**Te has pasado tres pueblos!** ¡Cómo se te ocurre decirle que se ha puesto como una una ballena!* • *You're out of order! What were you thinking about telling her she was like a whale!*

pasma *n.*

FILTH, PIGS, BACON

—*¡Larguémonos de aquí, que viene la **pasma!*** • *Let's get outta here! The pigs are coming!*

pasta *n.*

DOSH, CHEDDA, GREEN

—*Me he gastado una **pasta** en estos zapatos.* • *I splashed a load of dosh on these shoes.*

pata

1 meter la pata *loc.*

TO PUT ONE'S FOOT IN IT,
TO BALLS SOMETHING UP

—*Al decirle a Juan lo de la fiesta*

*has metido la **pata**. Lo sabes, ¿no?* • *You put your foot in it telling Juan about the party. Know what I mean?*

2 tener mala pata *loc.*

TO BE A JINX, TO BE A GAFF

—*Nunca juego a nada porque siempre **tengo** muy **mala pata.*** • *I never bet 'cos I'm a jinx.*

3 estirar la pata *loc.*

TO KICK THE BUCKET,
TO POP ONE'S CLOGS

—*¿Cuándo **estiró la pata** el capullo ese?* • *When did that prick pop his clogs?*

patada (sentar como una) *loc.*

TO GO DOWN LIKE A TON OF BRICKS

—*Le ha sentado como una **patada** que no le hayamos invitado. La próxima vez invítalo sin falta.* • *It went down like a ton of bricks when he found out that we didn't invite him. Next time you gotta invite him.*

patearse *v. prnl.*

TO WALK

—*Estoy hecha polvo, **me he pateado** toda la ciudad buscando unos zapatos.* • *I'm knackered, I've walked all over town looking for shoes.*

patilla (por la) *loc.*

FOR FREE, FOR NOTHING,
FOR NOWT

—*Entramos en el concierto **por la patilla**.* • *We got into the gig for nothing.*

FOR EXTRA COOLNESS YOU CAN GET YOUR SYNONYMS OUT AND SAY POR EL MORRO OR DE GORRA

patillero/a *adj.*
CHEESY, TACKY

—*Es bastante **patillero** el espectáculo: la bailaora y los músicos lo hacen bastante mal y el local es bastante cutre.* • *The show's pretty cheesy; the flamenco dancer and the musicians are crap and the place is tacky.*

pavo/a *n., adj.*
1 BLOKE, GEEZER, GUY

2 DIPPY

—*Me cae bien la novia de mi hermano, pero es un poco **pava**.* • *I like my brother's girlfriend but she's a bit dippy.*

pechonalidad *n.*
This is a nice bit of wordplay. **Pechos** are "breasts". **Personalidad** is "personality". Well, some guys like ladies with a big personality. Know what I mean?

—*Me encanta que las tías tengan mucha **pechonalidad*** • *I love women with a big personality.*

pedal *n.*
A PISS UP

—*Llevábamos un buen **pedal** anoche.* • *We had a right piss up last night.*

pedazo de *adv.*
STONKING BIG

—*¡**Pedazo de** cabrón estás hecho!* • *You stonking big asshole!*

pedo *n., adj.*
BLOOTERED, WAZZED, PISSED [UK], HAMMERED

—*Íbamos muy **pedo** el viernes ¿verdad?* • *We were hammered on Friday, weren't we?*

pedorro/a *n.*
DICKHEAD

—*Pasa de ella, colega, es una **pedorra**.* • *Never mind her, dude, she's a dickhead.*

pegar *v.*
1 TO BE A GOOD MATCH

—*Estos dos no **pegan** ni con cola. No creo que duren mucho.* • *That couple are not a good match. I don't give them much time.*

2 pegársela *v. prnl.*
TO CRASH

—*Se la ha pegado con la moto pero por suerte no le ha pasado nada.* • *He crashed his motorbike, luckily he didn't do himself any damage.*

pela (me la) *expr. (vul.)*
I DON'T GIVE A SHIT, I DON'T GIVE A TOSS

pelársela *v. prnl. (vul.)*
TO WHACK OFF, TO WANK

—*Se pasa el día pelándosela mirando pelis porno.* • *He spends day whacking off and watching pornos.*

película *n.*
A YARN

—*Dice que con lo que gane se comprará un piso y un deportivo. ¡A veces se monta unas películas!* • *He says with all the dough he makes he's gonna buy a flat and a sports car. He's been known to spin a few yarns.*

pelma *adj., n.*
A PAIN IN THE ASS

—*¿Viene el pelma de tu primo?* • *Is your pain in the ass cousin coming?*

pelo
1 a pelo *loc.*

NAKED OR WITHOUT SOMETHING, ON ITS OWN

—*Lo hicieron a pelo.* • *They did it without a johnny.*

2 de pelo en pecho *loc.*
VERY MACHO

—*Es un hombre de pelo en pecho.* • *He's a macho man.*

3 caérsele el pelo *loc.*
TO GET WHAT'S COMING

—*Se te va a caer el pelo cuando el jefe se entere de que la has cagado.* • *You're gonna get what's coming when the boss finds out you've ballsed it up.*

4 no tener pelos en la lengua *loc.*
TO BE MOUTHY

—*María no tiene pelos en la lengua, dice todo lo que piensa.* • *Maria's mouthy, she says what she thinks.*

5 no cortarse un pelo *loc.*
TO DO ANYTHING

—*Mark no se corta un pelo, se atreve con todo.* • *Mark would do anything.*

6 no tener un pelo de tonto/a *loc.*
TO BE BRAINY

—*Ya sé que no tienes un pelo de tonta, aunque a veces lo pareces, hija.* • *I know you're brainy, but sometimes you don't act it.*

7 tomar el pelo *loc.*

TO PULL SOMEBODY'S LEG,
TO HAVE SOMEBODY ON

—*Deja de* **tomarme el pelo** *que hoy no estoy para bromas.* • *Stop pulling my leg. I'm not in the mood.*

pelota *n.*

AN ARSELICKER,
A BROWN-NOSER

—*Eres un* **pelota**. • *You're a brown-noser.*

1 en pelotas *loc.*

IN THE BUFF, STARKERS

—*Espera, dame un minuto, que estoy* **en pelotas**. • *Hold on, I'll open the door in a minute, I'm in the buff.*

2 hacer la pelota *loc.*

TO BUTTER SOMEONE UP

—*¡No me* **hagas la pelota** *que no vas a conseguir nada!* • *Don't butter me up. You won't get anywhere!*

3 írsele la pelota *loc.*

TO LOSE IT, TO GO MENTAL

—*Le dijo al juez que había matado a su mujer porque* **se le había ido la pelota**. • *He told the judge he killed his wife 'cos he just lost it.*

4 (no) tener pelotas *loc.*

TO HAVE (THE) BALLS, TO HAVE (THE) BOLLOCKS

—*¡No* **tienes pelotas** *para hacerlo!* • *You don't have the bollocks to do it!*

5 tocar las pelotas *loc.*

TO GET ON ONE'S WICK
Literally to have your balls touched. In Spanish, if somebody "touches your balls", they get on your wick.

—*¡No me* **toques las pelotas**! • *Stop getting on my wick!*

pelotazo *n.*

1 A PISS UP

—*Yo paso de cogerme otro* **pelotazo** *como el del viernes. Mi cuerpo ya no está para estos trotes.* • *No more piss ups like Friday's for me. My body can't take it.*

pendón *n., adj.*

1 UP FOR THE PARTY

—*Marta es un* **pendón**. *No tiene horarios, sale de juerga casi todas las noches y cada día está con un chico diferente.* • *Marta's always up for the party. She's not one for timetables, out every night and always with a different bloke.*

2 A SLUT, A TART

—*Esa tía es un* **pendón**. *Se acuesta con cualquiera.* • *That bird's a slut. She doesn't care who she beds.*

peña (la) *n.*

THE GUYS, YOUR PALS,
PEOPLE (IN GENERAL)

—*Había mogollón de* **peña** *en el concierto de ayer.* • *Gig was mobbed yesterday.*

peñazo *n.*
SOMETHING THAT'S DEAD,
DEAD BORING

—*La clase de hoy ha sido un verdadero **peñazo**.* • *Today's class was
dead, dead boring.*

peor (lo) *loc.*
THE LOWEST OF THE LOW

—*Mi tío es **lo peor**. Ha dejado a
mi tía por una pava de 22 años.* •
*My uncle's the lowest of the low. He's
dumped my aunt for some twenty-
two year old bird.*

perrear *v.*
This verb comes from the musical
phenomenon **reggaetón**. This
reggaetón is a kind of hip hop, rap,
reggae fusion which also takes on
other Latin American influences.
Anyway, this type of dance emer-
ged called the **perreo** or **perrear**
in its verb form. It basically means
"do the doggy" which when wit-
nessed reminds one of two dogs
together, male behind the female.
In English we could describe it as
"grinding" or "booty dancing".

perrería *n.*
TO FUCK OVER

—*Te han hecho una buena **perre-
ría** en el curro.* • *They've really
fucked you over at work.*

peste, pestazo *n.*
A PONG, A MING

—*¡Qué **peste**! ¿A quién le canta el
alerón?* • *What a pong! Whose pits
are minging?*

peta *n.*
JOINT

—*¡Tío, pásame el **peta**!* • *Pass the
joint, mate!*

petado/a *adj.*
KNACKERED, SHATTERED

—*Me piro, estoy super**petada**.* • *I'm
gonna hit the road, I'm knackered.*

petar (a) *loc. adv.*
MOBBED, HEAVING

—*Estaba **a petar** el concierto.* •
The gig was heaving.

petardo/a *adj.*
CHEESY

—*Mi compañero de piso solo escucha música **petarda**: Gloria Gaynor, Village People...* • *My flatmate
only listens to cheesy music: Gloria
Gaynor, Village People...*

pez (estar) *loc.*
TO NOT KNOW SHIT

—**Estoy pez** en informática. • *I don't know shit about computers.*

pibón *n.*
A BABE, A FIT BIRD

—*Este garito esta lleno de* **pibones**, *aquí nos quedamos.* • *This boozer's full of babes, we're staying here.*

pifiarla *v.*
TO MUCK UP, TO BALLS UP, TO BLOW IT

—*Mierda,* **la he pifiado** *otra vez en el curro.* • *Shit, I've mucked it up again at work.*

pijo/a *adj., n.*
A PRENTENTIOUS GIT, A STUCK-UP GIT, SNOOTY

—*No sé cómo puedes salir con Borja, es super***pijo***.* • *I don't know how you can go out with Borja, he's so stuck-up.*

pilas (ponerse las) *loc.*
TO GET ONE'S FINGER OUT, TO MOVE ONE'S ASS

—*Tía,* **ponte las pilas** *que lo vas a catear todo.* • *Get your finger out. You're gonna flunk everything.*

pilila *n.*
WILLIE, TODGER, JOHN THOMAS

This is a word used especially with kids.

piltrafilla *n.*
LITTLE SHIT

—*¡Eh, tú,* **piltrafilla**, *apártate!* • *Hey, you little shit, stand aside!*

pillar *v.*
1 TO GET IT

—*¿Lo* **pillas** *o no?* • *Do you get it or not?*

2 TO SCORE DRUGS

—*¿Vas a* **pillar** *algo de costo para esta noche?* • *Are you gonna score some hash for tonight?*

3 TO SCORE, TO PULL, TO GET OFF WITH SOMEONE

—**¿Pillaste** *cacho anoche?* • *Did you pull last night?*

4 TO NICK (ARREST)

—*Me han dicho que han* **pillado** *al camello del barrio.* • *I heard the hood dealer got nicked.*

pinchar *v.*
1 TO BE ON THE DECKS, TO DJ

—*¿Quién* **pincha** *hoy en el Sidecar?* • *Who's on the decks at Sidecar 2nite?*

2 pinchar el teléfono *loc.*
TO BUG, TO TAP

—*Al alcalde le han* **pinchado el**

teléfono. • *The mayor's phone's been bugged.*

4 pincharse *v. prnl.*
TO SHOOT UP

—*Menos mal que Juan ya no se **pincha**.* • *At least Juan doesn't shoot up anymore.*

pino (en el quinto) *loc.*
IN THE MIDDLE OF NOWHERE

—*No tengo ganas de ir a su casa, vive **en el quinto pino**.* • *I can't be bothered going to this house. He lives in the middle of nowhere.*

JESUS CHRIST MAKES A REGULAR APPEARANCE IN SPANISH SLANG. SO, WE CAN ALSO SAY "WHERE JESUS LOST HIS HAT," DONDE CRISTO PERDIÓ EL GORRO

pinta(s) *n.*
LOOK, STATE

—*¡Vaya **pintas** que me llevas!* • *Look at the state of you!*

piñata *n.*
NASHERS (TEETH)

—*¡Vaya **piñata** que tiene!* • *What a set of nashers he's got!*

piño (pegarse un) *loc.*
TO COME OFF, TO CRASH

—*Se pegó un **piño** con la bici y volvió a casa todo ensangrentado.* • *He came off his bike and came home covered in blood.*

pirado/a *adj.*
BARKING MAD, BONKERS, OFF ONE'S HEAD, MENTAL

—*¡Tú estás **pirao** tío!* • *You're off your head, mate!*

pirarse *v. prnl.*
TO HIT THE ROAD, TO HEAD, TO HIT THE DOOR

—*Me **piro** a casa que estoy hecho una mierda.* • *I'm heading home, I'm shattered.*

pirula *n.*
1 WILLIE, TODGER, WINKLE

—*¡Deja de tocarte la **pirula**!* • *Stop touching your willie!*

2 A DING, A BANG

—*Acabas de hacer una **pirula** con el coche.* • *You've just given the car a ding.*

3 A TAB

—*¿Me pasas una **pirula**?* • *Give us a tab, will you?*

plantar *v.*
TO DUMP, TO CHUCK

—*A Marga la han vuelto a **plantar**.* • *Marga's been dumped again.*

2 dar plantón *loc.*
TO STAND SOMEBODY UP

—*A mi también me han dado **plantón**.* • *I've been stood up too.*

plasta *n., adj.*
A PAIN IN THE ASS

—*Ya sabía que tu amigo era pesadito pero nunca imaginé que lo era tanto. Dios, ¡qué **plasta**!* • *I already knew your mate was a bit heavy but I never imagined he was so bad. God, what a pain in the ass!*

pluma (tener) *loc.*
TO BE CAMP

—*El hermano de Javier solo tiene 12 años pero tiene mucha **pluma**.* • *Javier's brother's only 12 but he's already pretty camp.*

polvo *n.*
A BONK, A SHAG

1 echar un polvo *loc.*
TO HAVE A SHAG

—*Hace la tira que no echo un **polvo**.* • *I haven't had a shag in ages.*

2 tener un polvo *loc.*
TO BE FUCKABLE, TO BE SHAGGABLE

—*¡Esa piba tiene un buen **polvo**!* • *That bird's really shaggable!*

polla *n. (vul.)*
DICK, COCK, KNOB

pollo (montar un) *loc.*
TO GIVE OR TO GET A BOLLOCKING

—*Me han montado un **pollo** por nada.* • *I got a bollocking for nothing.*

porro *n.*
JOINT, DOOBIE

—*¡Pásame el **porro** colega!* • *Pass me the joint, dude!*

potar *v.*
TO PUKE, TO UPCHUCK, TO THROW UP, TO BOKE

—*¿Quién **ha potado** en el baño?* • *Who puked in the bath?*

potorro *n. (vul.)*
FANNY, PUSSY

potra (tener) *loc.*
TO BE JAMMY

—*¡Vaya **potra** que tenéis! Nadie os ha visto haciendo trampas.* • *You're so jammy! Nobody saw you cheating.*

primo/a *n., adj.*
FOOL

—*No sé cómo lo haces pero siempre estás haciendo el **primo**.* • *I don't know how you do it, you're always playing the fool.*

pringar *v.*
1 TO SLOG

—*Aquí solo **pringo** yo.* • *I'm the only one slogging here.*

2 pringado/a *n., adj.*
LOSER

—*¡Eres un **pringao**, tío!* • *You're a loser, man.*

privar *v.*
1 TO BOOZE

—*Estuvimos **privando** toda la noche.* • *We were boozing all night.*

2 priva *n.*
BOOZE, BEVVY

—*¿Llevamos **priva** a la fiesta?* • *Are we taking any bevvy to the party?*

¡puerta! *expr.*
GET OUT OF HERE

—*Si quieres, dale otra oportunidad pero a la mínima, **¡puerta!*** • *If you want, give him one more chance but one false move, get out of here!*

puesto/a *adj.*
STONED

—*Este tío va **puesto**. Mírale los ojos.* • *That guy's stoned. Look at his eyes.*

pulirse *v. prnl.*
TO BLOW

—*Me he **pulido** toda la pasta durante las vacaciones. No me queda ni un duro.* • *I've blown all my dough during my holidays. I'm skint.*

pulpo *n.*
This literally means "octopus" and refers to the sleazy kind of guy who can't keep his hands to himself when it comes to the birds or chicks. The bird or chick is not normally in accordance with such physical attention.

—*¡Las manos quietas, **pulpo**!* *Keep your hands to yourself, creep!*

punto *n.*
1 A FUNNY REMARK, A QUIP, TO HIT THE NAIL ON THE HEAD

—*¡Eso ha sido un **punto**! ¡Un **puntazo**, sí señor!* • *You've hit the nail in the head. Yeah, man. On the head.*

2 coger el puntillo *loc.*

TO BE TIPSY, TO GET TIPSY

—*Anoche al final sin quererlo ni beberlo nos **cogimos el puntillo**, ¿verdad?* • *Last night without wanting to or drinking so much we got a bit tipsy, didn't we?*

3 darle el puntazo *loc.*

TO LOSE IT

—*Le dio el puntazo y nos dejo allí tirados.* • *He just lost it and left us there high and dry.*

4 y punto *expr.*

AND THAT'S IT, RIGHT!, (MEANING IT'S ALL OVER)

—*Si no te gusta, se lo dices **y punto**. Ya lo entenderá.* • *If you don't like it, just tell him and that's it. He'll understand.*

puta madre (de) *loc.*

ACE, COOL, THE DOG'S BOLLOCKS

—*Sandra es una tía **de puta madre**. Nunca te deja tirada.* • *Sandra's ace. She never lets you down.*

IF YOU REALLY FEEL STRONGLY ABOUT IT, YOU CAN SAY DE PUTÍSIMA MADRE, WHICH IS MORE EMPHATIC. SOMETIMES ONE HAS TO REALLY SAY WHAT ONE MEANS, AND FEEL GOOD ABOUT IT

putada *n.*

A BUMMER, A PISSER

—*¡Qué **putada** lo del piso! ¿Y ahora qué vas a hacer?* • *What a bummer about the flat! What are you gonna do now?*

putear *v.*

1 TO FUCK SOMEBODY OVER

—*Este año voy a **putearlo** mucho. Voy a ir a por él desde el primer día.* • *This year I'm really gonna fuck him over. I'm going for him from day one.*

2 puteado/a *adj.*

FUCKED OFF, PISSED OFF

—*La verdad es que voy a dejarlo porque me tienen muy **puteado**.* • *The truth is I'm gonna leave 'cos I'm really fucked off with them.*

putero *n.*

A MAN WHO REGULARLY FREQUENTS A WHORE

—*Dicen que el profe de mates es un **putero**. ∥No, no creo. No tiene pinta.* • *I heard the maths teacher frequents whores. ∥Nah! He doesn't look the type.*

quedada _n._
A RENDEZVOUS

—*Hemos convocado una **quedada** por internet para hacer un botellón en la playa.* • *We've set up a rendezvous by internet for a piss up on the beach.*

quedarse _v. prnl._
1 quedarse con algo
TO GET IT

—*¿**Te has quedado con algo** de lo que ha dicho?* • *Did you get anything that he said?*

2 quedarse con alguien
TO TAKE THE PISS, TO TAKE THE MICKEY

—*¿**Te estás quedando** conmigo?* • *Are you taking the piss?*

3 TO BE AWAY WITH THE FAIRIES

—*Se ha **quedado** pa' llá. No se empana de nada.* • *He's away with the fairies. He just doesn't get it.*

quemar _v._
TO BURN OUT

—*Este curro me está **quemando** mogollón.* • *This job's really burning me out.*

quillo/a _n._
A CHAV

—*Esto está lleno de **quillos**.* • *This place is full of chavs.*

que me quiten lo bailao _expr._
IT WAS WORTH IT

—*Me fui de fiesta y llegué sin dormir al avión, pero **que me quiten lo bailao**.* • *I went out on the town, got to the plane with no sleep, but it was sure worth it !*

The expression is often used when you turn up for work or something important the next day - hung-over, knackered due to no sleep and generally feeling like shit - but the satisfaction you feel because of the previous night's action far outweighs your current physical state.

rajar _v._

1 TO TALK SOMEBODY DOWN, TO TEAR STRIPS OFF SOMEBODY

—_¡Ya vale de **rajar** de todo el mundo! Que tú tampoco eres perfecto, ¿eh?_ • _Quit talking everybody down! You're not perfect, are you?_

2 rajado/a _adj., n._
CHICKEN

—_¡Vaya **rajado**! Mira que suspender la fiesta por miedo a los vecino._ • _That's so chicken calling the party off because of the neighbours!_

3 rajarse _v. prnl._
TO GO BACK ON ONE'S WORD, TO CHICKEN OUT

—_Al final **se rajó** y suspendió la fiesta._ • _He went back on his word and called the party off._

rascar _v._
TO GET SOMETHING OUT OF

—_Vámonos, que aquí ya no hay nada que **rascar**._ • _We're outta here. We can't get anything out of this._

raya _n._

1 A LINE (COKE)

—_Entré al baño y allí todo el mundo se estaba metiendo **rayas**._ • _I went into the john and they were all doing lines._

2 pasarse de la raya _loc._
TO GO OVERBOARD

—_**Te pasaste de la raya** en mi fiesta._ • _You went overboard at my party._

rayar _v._

1 TO PISS SOMEONE OFF, TO GET ON SOMEBODY'S TITS

—_Me estás **rayando** mogollón con tus historias._ • _You're getting on my tits with your wind up._

2 rayarse _v. prnl._
TO HAVE OR TO GET A HAMSTER WHEEL BRAIN

—_No **te rayes** tanto, no merece la pena._ • _Don't get a hamsterwheel brain, it's not worth it._

rebotarse _v. prnl._
TO GET PISSED OFF

—_**Se rebotó** mogollón conmigo por una chorrada._ • _She got so pissed off with me over nothing._

regadera (estar como una) _loc._

TO BE NUTS, TO BE OFF ONE'S HEAD, TO BE MENTAL

—**Estás como una regadera,** pero me caes muy bien. • You're nuts, but I like you.

regatear _v._

TO HAGGLE

—Me encanta ir con Rosa a los mercadillos porque sabe **regatear**. • I love going to markets with Rosa 'cos she knows how to haggle.

repatear _v._

TO PISS SOMEONE OFF

—Me **repatea** que le hayan dado el trabajo a ella. • It really pisses me off that she got the job.

resaca, resacón _n._

HANGOVER

—¡No puedo salir del sobre, tengo un **resacón** de la leche! • I can't get out of this pit, I've got a stonking, great hangover!

rollo _n., adj._

1 SOMETHING OR SOMEONE DEAD BORING

—¡Joder, tío! ¡Qué **rollo** de clase! • Oh, man! What a dead boring lesson!

2 A ONE NIGHT STAND, A FLING

—¿Qué tal tu nueva novia? //No es mi novia, solo es un **rollo**. • How's your new girlfriend? //She's not my girlfriend, it's just a fling.

3 buen/mal rollo _loc._

GOOD OR BAD VIBE

—En el curro hay muy **mal rollo**. • There are bad vibes at work.

4 rollazo _n., adj._

DEAD, DEAD BORING

—¡Qué **rollazo** de peli! • What a dead, dead boring film.

rosco (no comerse un) _loc._

THE SAD ACT OF NOT PULLING

—**No me comí un rosco** en la fiesta del viernes. • I didn't pull at the party on Friday.

rular _v._

1 TO GO (MACHINE)

—Este cacharro no **rula** bien. • This banger doesn't go.

2 TO ROLL A JOINT

—Ya **rulo** yo el porro, que tú no tienes ni idea. • I'll roll the joint 'cos you're useless.

3 TO PASS THE JOINT

—¡Oye, ya vale de monopolizar el porrito, que **rule** de una vez! • Hey, stop hogging the joint and pass the grass.

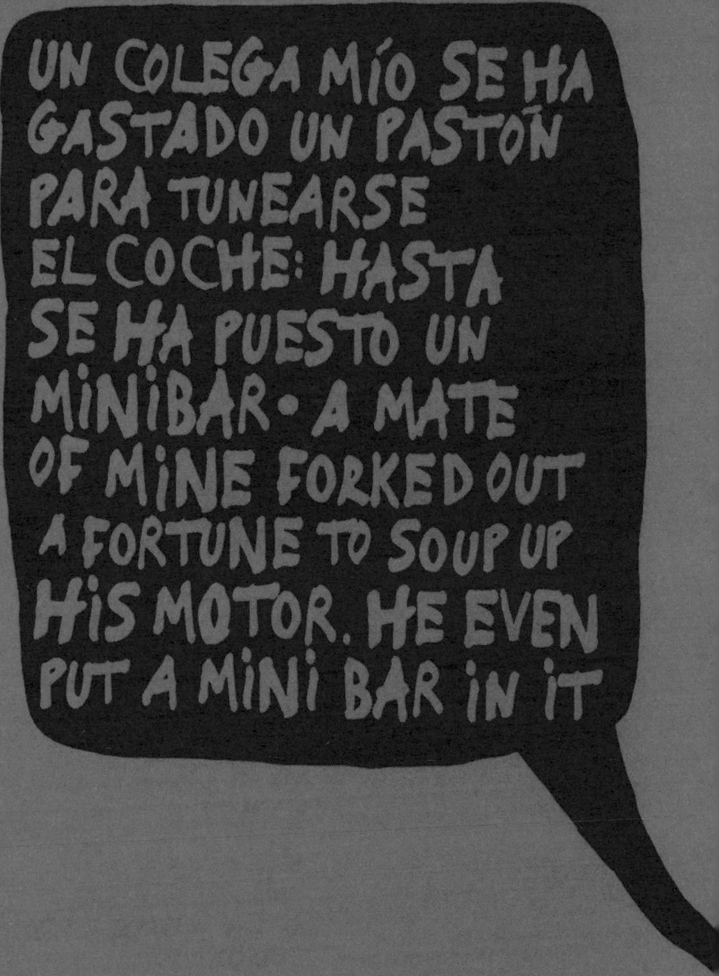
UN COLEGA MÍO SE HA GASTADO UN PASTÓN PARA TUNEARSE EL COCHE: HASTA SE HA PUESTO UN MINIBAR •
A MATE OF MINE FORKED OUT A FORTUNE TO SOUP UP HIS MOTOR. HE EVEN PUT A MINI BAR IN IT

sablazo *n.*

A RIP OFF

—*No vayas a ese restaurante; te van a meter un **sablazo** de la hostia.* • *Don't go to that restaurant, the prices are a total rip off.*

saco (a) *loc.*

GOOD AND PROPER, TO HAVE A RIGHT OLD SOMETHING (A LOT)

—*Cuando salgo con mis colegas privamos **a saco**.* • *When I go out with my mates we have a right old booze up.*

salido/a *adj., n.*

1 HORNY, RANDY

—*Estás más **salido** que un viejo verde.* • *You're hornier than a dirty old man.*

2 A HORNY BASTARD

—*Ten cuidado con Manu que tiene fama de ser un **salido**.* • *Careful with Manu, they say he's a horny bastard.*

salir *v.*

1 TO GO OUT WITH

—*¿Sabes que Víctor está **saliendo** con Ana?* • *Do you know that Víctor's going out with Ana?*

2 salir por patas *loc.*

TO HIT THE DOOR

—*Tuvimos que **salir por patas** porque casi zurran a Enric.* • *We had to hit the door 'cos Enric nearly got a doing.*

3 salirle el tiro por la culata *loc.*

TO COME OUT ARSE OVER TIT

—*Si no estás muy bien preparado para este trabajo, te puede **salir el tiro por la culata**.* • *If you're not really ready to do this job, it can come out arse over tit.*

4 salirse *v. prnl.*

TO ACE, TO FLY HIGH

—*Benicio del Toro **se sale** en el "Che".* • *Benicio del Toro flies high in "Che".*

IF IT'S REALLY GOOD AND YOU WANT TO REPEAT YOURSELF, USE THIS SYNONYM: LO BORDA

saque *n.*

THE ABILITY TO WOLF
SOMETHING DOWN OR TO
TUCK SOMETHING AWAY OR
TO POLISH SOMETHING OFF

—*¡Qué* **saque** *tienes, bebes más que un cosaco!* • *You certainly wolf it down, you drink like a fish.*

seco/a *adj.*

1 THIRSTY, DRY

—*Vamos a tomar una birrita; estoy* **superseca.** • *Let's get a drink, I'm mega dry.*

2 SKINT

—*Estoy* **seco,** *tío. ¿Me puedes dar algo de pasta?* • *I'm skint, mate. Can you give me some dosh?*

3 SKINNY

—*Tu hermana está muy* **seca.** *¿No será anoréxica?* • *Your sister's really skinny. She's not anorexic, is she?*

segurata *n.*

BOUNCER

—*El* **segurata** *de ayer era un gilipollas; no nos dejó pasar.* • *That bouncer from yesterday was a real prick, he didn't let us in.*

sembrado/a *adj.*

1 OUT OF ORDER

—*Tío has estado* **sembrado** *al preguntarle por su madre: ¿no sabías que falleció hace un mes?* • *Man,*

you were right out of order asking about her mum. Don't you know she died a month ago?

ORIGINALLY **SEMBRADO** MEANT TO BE WITTY. THESE DAYS IT'S USED TO IRONIC EFFECT MEANING OUT OF ORDER

2 ON A ROLL

—*Estoy* **sembrado.** *Llevo tres exámenes seguidos aprobados.* • *I'm on a roll. I've passed three exams.*

sinpa (hacer un) *loc.*

TO DO A RUNNER, TO LEG IT

—*No me extraña que no os deje pasar si siempre que podéis hacéis un* **sinpa.** • *I'm not surprised he didn't let you in. Whenever you can, you do a runner.*

sobar *v.*

1 TO KIP, TO DOSS

—*Esta noche* **sobamos** *en casa de Raquel.* • *We're dossing at Raquel's tonight.*

2 TO GROPE

—*Las manos quietas, que no me gusta que me* **soben.** • *Keep your hands to yourself, stop groping me!*

3 sobado/a *adj.*

KNACKERED, GROGGY,
SHATTERED

—*¡Estoy muy **sobao**, me voy a la piltra!* • *I'm totally knackered, I'm going to my pit!*

WORN-OUT, PLAYED-OUT, SO YESTERDAY

—*¡Ese chiste está muy **sobao**!* • *That joke is so yesterday!*

sobón/a *adj.*
TOUCHY-FEELY

—*Tío, estás un poco **sobón** hoy.* • *Dude, you're a bit touchy-feely today.*

sobrado/a (ir de) *loc.*
TO BE FULL OF ONESELF

—*Una cosa es ser muy bueno en algo y otra es **ir de sobrao**.* • *One thing is to be good at something, and being full of yourself is another.*

sobre *n.*
PIT, SACK (BED)

—*Me voy al **sobre** que mañana curro temprano.* • *I'm going to my pit 'cos I'm up early for work in the morning.*

soplar *v.*
1 TO NICK, TO GANK

—*Me han **soplado** la cartera en el metro.* • *I got my wallet ganked on the subway.*

2 TO DOWN

—*Nos **soplamos** una botella de whisky entre los dos.* • *We downed*

a bottle of whisky between the two of us.

3 TO RAT ON, TO FINK ON, TO FINK SOMEONE OUT, TO GRASS ON

—*Alguien les **sopló** dónde teníamos escondido el alijo.* • *Somebody ratted on us and told them where the stash was hidden.*

4 soplón/a *n.*
GRASS, RAT

—*Cogieron al sospechoso porque los maderos tenían un **soplón**.* • *They brought in the suspect because the pigs had a grass.*

subidón *n.*
A HIGH

—*Solo de pensar en ganar el premio me entra el **subidón**.* • *Just thinking about winning the prize gives me a high.*

sudar *v.*
TO NOT GIVE A TOSS

—*Me la **suda** que no haya venido. ¡Allá él!* • *I don't give a toss if he hasn't come. His problem!*

super *adv.*
DEAD, MEGA
A very common adverb among the young and hip, everything is **super** something.

—*Esto es **super**chungo.* • *This is dead dodgy.*

tacos *n. pl.*
YEARS

—*Mi viejo hoy cumple 60 **tacos**.*
• *My old man's sixty-years-old today.*

taja *n.*
A PISS UP

—*Pillamos una buena **taja** el viernes.* • *We had a right old piss up on Friday.*

tajada (sacar) *loc.*
TO GET SOMETHING OUT OF, TO GET OR WANT A PIECE OF THE ACTION

—*Mario siempre **saca tajada** de todo.* • *Mario always wants a piece of the action.*

talego *n.*
1 THE NICK, THE SLAMMER

—*Estuvo tres meses en el **talego**.*
• *He spent three months in the slammer.*

2 DOSH, CHEDDA
In the time of **pesetas** this was the green **1000 peseta** note, now it could be any note or any quantity of money. We can call it "chedda", "dosh", "green", etc.

—*¿Me prestas unos **talegos**, tío?*
• *Can I cadge some dosh, man?*

talibán *n.*
AN AUTHORITIVE PERSON, A FASCIST

—*El novio de mi vecina es un **talibán**, a la pobre no le deja hacer nada.* • *My neighbour's bloke's a right fascist, he doesn't let the poor girl do anything.*

tela (tener) *loc.*
1 TO BE A HEAVY SITUATION

—*El asunto **tiene** mucha **tela**.*
• *This is a heavy situation.*

2 ¡vaya tela! *expr.*
THIS IS HEAVY!, WOW!, LOOK AT THAT!

teta (pasarlo) *loc.*
1 TO WHOOP IT UP

—*Lo pasamos **teta** en la fiesta.*
• *We really whooped it up at the party.*

2 tetas *n. pl.*

TITS, JUBBLIES, JUGS, BOOBS, MAMS

—*¡Vaya **tetas** que tiene esa!* • *Oh man, look at the jugs on that.*

tío/a *n.*

MATE, DUDE, BLOKE, GEEZER

—*¿Qué pasa, **tío**?* • *Wassup, dude?*

tigre (oler a) *loc.*

TO MING OF BO

—*Abrid una ventana, por favor, que aquí **huele a tigre** que tira.* • *Open the window, please! It mings of BO in here.*

tipo/a *n.*

BLOKE, GUY

—*Hay un **tipo** muy chungo en la puerta.* • *There's a real dodgy bloke at the door.*

tiquismiquis *adj.*

FUSSY

—*¡No seas tan **tiquismiquis** y cómetelo!* • *Don't be so fussy and eat it!*

tira (hacer la) *loc.*

FOR YONKS, FOR AGES

—*¡Joder! **Hacía la tira** que no nos habíamos visto. Qué mala pinta tienes, no te había reconocido.* • *Bloody hell! We haven't seen each other for yonks. You look like shit, I didn't recognise you.*

tirado/a *adj.*

1 DIRT CHEAP

—*Esos zapatos están **tirados**.* • *Those shoes are dirt cheap.*

2 EASY-PEASY, CAKE

—*El examen estaba **tirado**. Saqué un 9.* • *The exam was total cake. I got a 9.*

3 dejar tirado/a *loc.*

TO LEAVE SOMEBODY HIGH AND DRY

—*¡De qué vais, tíos! ¡Me dejasteis **tirada** en el último bar!* • *Fuck's sake guys! You left me high and dry in that last pub!*

tirar los tejos *loc.*

TO GIVE SOMEBODY THE COME ON

—*Le **tiré los tejos** toda la noche y total para nada.* • *I gave her the come on all night and all for nothing.*

tirarse *v. prnl. (vul.)*

TO BONK, TO KNOB, TO SHAG SOMEONE

—*Este tío es un salido, intenta **tirarse** a todo lo que se mueve.* • *This guy's horny, he'd shag anything that moved.*

tocapelotas *n.*
A PAIN IN THE ASS

—¡David es un **tocapelotas**! • David's a pain in the ass!

tocho *n.*
1 A BIG THICK BOOK

—Me estoy leyendo un **tocho** de 900 páginas. • I'm reading this big, thick 900-page book.

2 poner los tochos *loc.*
TO TWO-TIME, TO CHEAT ON

—Si le **pones los tochos** te mato. • If you two-time her I'll kill you.

YOU CAN ALSO SAY
PONER LOS CUERNOS.
BUT, YOU SHOULDN'T
DO IT, SHOULD YOU?

tomate *n.*
ARGY BARGY, A DING DONG

—¡Aquí hay **tomate**! • There's a bit of argy-bargy here!

tope *adv.*
1 DEAD (VERY)

—¡Es **tope** guay! • It's dead cool!

2 a tope *loc.*
TO THE FULL, FULL ON

—Hay que vivir la vida **a tope**. • You've gotta live life to the full.

3 hasta los topes *loc.*
MOBBED, HEAVING

—El concierto estaba **hasta los topes**. • The concert was heaving.

toque (dar un) *loc.*
1 TO HOLLA, TO GIVE A BELL

—**Dame un toque** cuando sepas algo. • Just holla me when you know.

2 TO GIVE SOMEBODY A KICK UP THE ASS

—**Dale un toque** a Pelayo, que últimamente se está colgando mucho. • Give Pelayo a kick up the ass, he's been slacking lately.

tortillera *n.*
DYKE

—¡Deja de mirar a mi chica, **tortillera**! • Stop eyeing up my bird, you dyke!

tostar *v.*
TO BURN CDS

—**He tostado** todos estos CDs para ti. • I've burnt all these CDs 4U.

tostón *n.*
A PISS BORING THING, A REAL BORE, A DRAG, A SLEEPER

—La conferencia de ayer fue un **tostón**. • Yesterday's conference was piss boring.

total _adv._

TO CUT A LONG STORY SHORT,
TO SKIP TO THE END

—_Yo no perdería el tiempo intentando convencerle._ **Total** _no va a ir._ •
I wouldn't waste time trying to convince him. To cut a long story short, he's not gonna go.

tranqui _expr._

TAKE IT EASY, CHILLAX

—_¡Eh,_ **tranqui**_, chavales, o voy a empezar a repartir!_ • _Hey, take it easy, guys or you'll get it!_

trapichear _v._

TO DEAL (DRUGS)

—_Le han metido en el talego por_ **trapichear** _en la puerta del insti._
• _He got nicked for dealing at the school gates._

travelo _n._

TRANNY

—_Por la zona del estadio hay muchos_ **travelos**_._ • _There're loads of trannies up by the stadium._

tripi _n._

A TAB (ACID)

—_¿Tienes_ **tripis**_?_ • _Got any tabs?_

trola _n._

1 A WHOPPER, A PORKY (LIE)

—_Vaya_ **trola** _que nos ha contado tu hermano. No se lo cree ni él que sale con una modelo._ • _What a whopper your brother told us! Is he fuck going out with a model._

2 trolero/a _n., adj._

GOBSHITE

—_¡De ése no te creas nada que es un_ **trolero**_!_ • _Don't believe anything that gobshite says!_

truño _n._

CRAP

—_¡Vaya_ **truño** _de peli!_ • _What a crap flick!_

tunear _v._

TO SOUP UP

—_Un colega mío se ha gastado un pastón para_ **tunearse** _el coche: hasta se ha puesto un minibar._ •
A mate of mine forked out a fortune to soup up his motor. He even put a mini bar in it.

turca (pillar una) _loc._

TO GET PISSED, TROLLIED, WAZZED, BLOOTERED, BLOTTO, HAMMERED, WELLIED

—**Pillaron una** _buena_ **turca** _en la fiesta._ • _They got really pissed at the party._

tutiplén (a) _loc._

SHITLOADS

—_Había comida_ **a tutiplén** _en la fiesta._ • _There was shitloads of grub at the party._

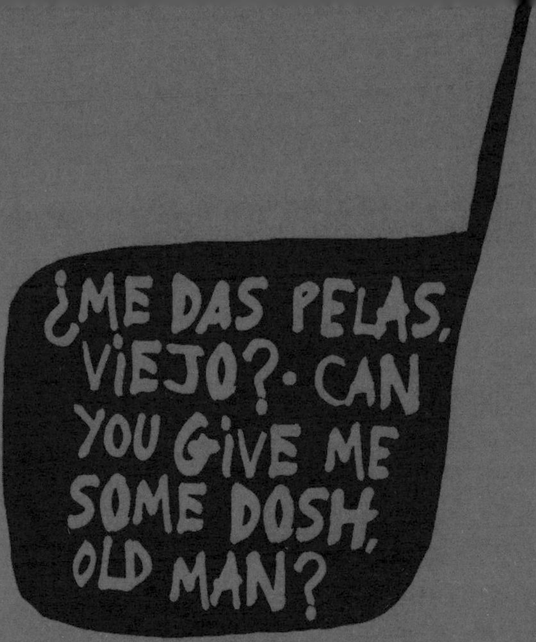
¿ME DAS PELAS, VIEJO?. CAN YOU GIVE ME SOME DOSH, OLD MAN?

último (lo) *loc.*

THE LAST STRAW

—*Esto es lo último; encima se enfa-da ella.* • *This is the last straw. She even got angry.*

ultra *n.*

HOOLIGAN

—*Los ultras del Valencia la liaron mazo después del partido contra el Sevilla.* • *The Valencia hooligans went wild after the game against Sevilla.*

urbanita *n.*

A CITY BOY, A CITY GIRL

—*El tío no sale nunca de Madrid. Es 100% urbanita.* • *The guy's never left Madrid. He's a total city boy.*

vacilar *v.*

1 TO WIND SOMEONE UP, TO KID, TO TAKE THE MICKEY

—*Tu primo me estuvo vacilando toda la noche. Al principio era diver-tido pero acabé hasta los huevos de él y de sus bromitas.* • *Your cousin was winding me up all night. It was funny at first but in the end I was pissed off with him and his stupid jokes.*

2 vacilón/a *n.*

JOKER, WISE GUY, CLOWN, TEASE

—*Tu novio es un vacilón, nunca va en serio.* • *Your boyfriend's a right joker, he doesn't take anything seriously.*

veleta *n.*

Literally it means "weather cock". So, this refers to somebody who has so many changes of opinion that their position moves more than a weather cock. A very fickle person indeed.

—*Eres un **veleta** siempre estás cambiando de opinión.* • *You're so fickle, you're always changing your mind.*

ventilarse *v. prnl.*
TO BLOW, TO FINISH OFF

—*El alcalde dice que no hay pasta para construir el pavellón. Claro, como **se ventilaron** toda la pasta en el nuevo ayuntamiento.* • *The mayor says there's no dough to build the arena. Of course, they blew it all on the new city hall.*

verde
1 estar verde *loc.*
TO BE GREEN

—*Fernando **está** un poco **verde** para debutar con el primer equipo.* • *Fernando is a bit green to make his debut in the first team.*

2 poner verde *loc.*
TO SLAG OFF

—*Me **puso verde** delante de todo el mundo y se quedó tan ancha la tía.* • *She slagged me off in front of everybody and she didn't give a toss.*

víbora *n.*
A BITCH

—*¡Menuda **víbora** la vecina de abajo!* • *The neighbour downstairs is a real bitch!*

vidilla (dar) *loc.*
TO SPRUCE UP

—*Vamos a poner un par de fotos en la web para **darle** un poco de **vidilla**.* • *We're gonna put a couple of photos up on the website to spruce it up a bit.*

vidorra *n.*
THE GOOD LIFE, TO LIVE IT UP, TO HAVE IT LARGE

—*Desde que dejaste ese curro, menuda **vidorra** que te pegas.* • *Since you quit that job, you've been enjoying the good life.*

viejo/a *n.*
1 THE OLD MAN (DAD), THE OLD DEAR (MUM)

—*¿Me das pelas, **viejo**?* • *Can you give me some dosh, old man?*

2 viejo verde
DIRTY OLD MAN

—*Mi vecino es un **viejo verde**. Está totalmente obsesionado con las chicas jóvenes.* • *My neighbour's a dirty old man. He's totally obsessed with the young birds.*

voleo (a) *loc.*
OFF THE TOP OF MY HEAD, TO WING IT

—*No tenía ni idea de la mitad de las preguntas del examen. Casi todas las contesté **a voleo**.* • *I didn't have a clue how to answer half the questions in the exam. I just winged it.*

ya vale *expr.*

ENOUGH IS ENOUGH

—**Ya vale** de pedir más dinero. Apáñate con lo que tienes. • *Enough is enough. I'm not giving you anymore money. You'll have to get by on what you've got.*

ya te vale *expr.*

SHAME ON YOU

—*Joder, pavo,* **ya te vale**. *Mira que no avisar de que no venías.* • *Bloody hell, man. Shame on you. You should've said you weren't coming.*

ya ves *expr.*

THAT'S NOTHING

—*Ayer corrí 2 km, tío. Estoy petao.* // *¿2 km?* **Ya ves,** *tampoco es tanto.* • *Yesterday I ran 2 km, man. I'm shattered.* // *2 km? That's nothing.*

yayo/a *n.*

GRANDAD, GRANNY

—*El* **yayo** *me ha regalado un iPod y la* **yaya** *un diccionario de inglés.* // *¡Qué monos!* • *Grandad gave me an iPod and granny gave me an English dictionary.* // *That's nice!*

yogurín *n.*

TOY BOY

—*Dicen que Marta está saliendo con un* **yogurín**. • *I heard Marta's got a toy boy.*

yonqui *n.*

JUNKIE

—*Esta zona está llena de* **yonquis**. • *This place is full of junkies.*

yuyu

1 dar yuyu *loc.*

TO FREAK SOMEBODY OUT, TO GIVE SOMEBODY THE CREEPS

—*La magia negra me* **da yuyu**. • *Black magic gives me the creeps.*

2 dar un yuyu *loc.*

TO BLACK OUT

—*A una compañera de trabajo le* **dio un yuyu** *ayer por la tarde mientras trabajaba. La tuvieron que ingresar y todo.* • *My workmate blacked out yesterday afternoon while she was working. They even had to take her to hospital and everything.*

zamparse *v. prnl.*

TO POLISH OFF, TO WOLF
DOWN, TO TUCK AWAY

—*¡Te lo has **zampado** todo! ¡Tienes un agujero en el estómago!* • *You've certainly polished that off! You've got a bottomless belly, mate!*

zarpa (meter la) *loc.*

TO GET ONE'S PAWS ON
SOMETHING

—*Te encanta **meter la zarpa** en todo.* • *You love getting your paws on everything.*

zipizape *n.*

ARGY BARGY, A DING DONG

—*Se armó un **zipizape** en las escaleras, casi llegaron a las manos.* • *There was a bit of argy bargy on the stairs, it almost came to fisticuffs.*

zombi *n.*

BE LIKE A ZOMBIE

—*Yo todas las mañanas voy **zombi** al curro.* • *I go to work like a zombie every morning.*

zorra *n.*

A SLUT

—*¡Eres una **zorra**, aléjate de mi novio!* • *You slut! Stay away from my boyfriend!*

zumbado/a *adj.*

MENTAL, MAD

—*Ese tío está muy **zumbao**. Yo no le haría mucho caso.* • *That guy's mental. I wouldn't listen to him.*

zurrar *v.*

TO BEAT UP, TO DECK,
TO FLOOR

—*Me **zurraron** unos macarras en el metro.* • *I got beat up by some hoodies on the underground.*

zurullo *n.*

TURD WITH A LIFE JACKET

—*¡Qué asco! Hay un **zurullo** enorme en el váter. El que lo haya hecho que lo solucione.* • *Barfaroni! There's a humungous turd with a life jacket in the toilet. Could the guilty one deal with it?*